P9-CWE-325

PRESENTED TO

_____

FROM

_____

MAX LUCADO

FEAR NOT

For I Am with You Always

PROMISE BOOK

THOMAS NELSON
Since 1798

NASHVILLE   MEXICO CITY   RIO DE JANEIRO

FEAR NOT

God Is with You

*The L*ORD *spoke his word to Abram in a vision:*
"Abram, don't be afraid. I will defend you,
and I will give you a great reward."

GENESIS 15:1 NCV

∿

[Jesus] said to them, "Why are you troubled?
And why do doubts arise in your hearts?
Behold My hands and My feet, that it is I Myself."

LUKE 24:38–39

∿

Joseph of Arimathea came,
a prominent member of the Council,
who himself was waiting for the kingdom of God;
and he gathered up courage and went in before Pilate,
and asked for the body of Jesus.

MARK 15:43 NASB

When fear shapes our lives, safety becomes our god. When safety becomes our god, we worship the risk-free life. Can the safety-lover do anything great? Can the risk-averse accomplish noble deeds? for God? for others? No.

The fear-filled cannot love deeply. Love is risky.

They cannot give to the poor. Benevolence has no guarantee of return.

The fear-filled cannot dream wildly. What if their dreams sputter and fall from the sky?

The worship of safety emasculates greatness. No wonder Jesus wages such a war against fear.

Fearless

Be strong and brave.
Don't be afraid . . . and don't be frightened,
because the LORD your God will go with you.
He will not leave you or forget you.

DEUTERONOMY 31:6 NCV

~

Be anxious for nothing, but in everything
by prayer and supplication,
with thanksgiving, let your requests
be made known to God; and the peace of God,
which surpasses all understanding,
will guard your hearts and minds
through Christ Jesus.

PHILIPPIANS 4:6–7

*Stop being
perpetually
uneasy (anxious
and worried) about
your life.*

Christ cautions us against taking up membership in the fraternity of Woe-Be-Me: "Therefore I tell you, stop being perpetually uneasy (anxious and worried) about your life" (Matthew 6:25 AMP).

Jesus doesn't condemn legitimate concern for responsibilities but rather the continuous mind-set that dismisses God's presence. Destructive anxiety subtracts God from the future, faces uncertainties with no faith, and tallies up the challenges of the day without entering God into the equation.

Worry is the darkroom where negatives become glossy prints.

Fearless

The LORD appeared to him that night and said,
"I am the God of your father Abraham. Don't be afraid,
because I am with you."

GENESIS 26:24 NCV

~~~

The Lord spoke to Paul in the night by a vision,
"Do not be afraid, but speak, and do not keep silent;
for I am with you."

ACTS 18:9–10

~~~

Where can I flee from Your presence? . . .
If I take the wings of the morning,
And dwell in the uttermost parts of the sea,
Even there Your hand shall lead me,
And Your right hand shall hold me.

PSALM 139:7, 9–10

> *"I am with you always, even to the end of the age."*
>
> MATTHEW 28:20

Mark it down. You will never go where God is not. You may be transferred, enlisted, commissioned, reassigned, or hospitalized, but—brand this truth on your heart—you can never go where God is not.

Every Day Deserves a Chance

He satisfies the longing soul,
And fills the hungry soul with goodness.

PSALM 107:9

Don't be afraid of what they fear;
do not dread those things.
But remember that the LORD All-Powerful is holy.

ISAIAH 8:12–13 NCV

The angel answered and said to the women,
"Do not be afraid, for I know that you seek Jesus who was
crucified. He is not here; for He is risen, as He said."

MATTHEW 28:5–6

Oversized and rude, fear is unwilling to share the heart with happiness. Happiness complies. Do you ever see the two together?

Can one be happy and afraid at the same time?

Clear thinking and afraid?

Confident and afraid?

Merciful and afraid?

No. Fear is the big bully in the high school hallway: brash, loud, and unproductive. For all the noise fear makes and room it takes, fear does little good.

Fearless

[The angel] said, "O man greatly beloved, fear not!
Peace be to you; be strong, yes, be strong!"

DANIEL 10:19

~~

Even if you should suffer for righteousness' sake,
you are blessed. "And do not be afraid of
their threats, nor be troubled."

1 PETER 3:14

~~

There stood by me this night an angel of the God to whom I
belong and whom I serve, saying, "Do not be afraid, Paul; you
must be brought before Caesar."

ACTS 27:23–24

"The angel of the LORD encamps all around those who fear Him, and delivers them" (Psalm 34:7). Let that truth lower your anxiety level! The wealthiest of the world don't have the protection God's servants give you.

God sends his best troops to oversee your life. Imagine the president assigning his Secret Service to protect you, telling his agents to motorcade your car through traffic and safeguard you through crowds. How would you sleep if you knew D.C.'s finest guarded your door? How will you sleep knowing heaven's finest are doing just that? You are not alone. Receive God's lordship over your life. Heaven's many, mighty angels watch over you.

Come Thirsty

Be of good courage, and He shall strengthen your heart,
all you who hope in the LORD.

PSALM 31:24

~

Do not fear, little flock,
for it is your Father's good pleasure
to give you the kingdom.

LUKE 12:32

~

Say to those who are fearful-hearted,
"Be strong, do not fear!
Behold, your God . . .
will come and save you."

ISAIAH 35:4

Fear never wrote a symphony or poem, negotiated a peace treaty, or cured a disease.

Fear never pulled a family out of poverty or a country out of bigotry.

Fear never saved a marriage or a business.

Courage did that. Faith did that.

People who refused to consult or cower to their timidities did that. But fear itself? Fear herds us into a prison and slams the doors.

Wouldn't it be great to walk out?

Fearless

Suppose you could relive your life without any guilt, lust, vengeance, insecurity, or fear. Would you be different?

God changes the man by changing the mind. And how does it happen? As Christ dominates your thoughts, he changes you from one degree of glory to another until—hang on!—you are ready to live with him.

Heaven is the land of sinless minds. Absolute trust. No fear or anger. Shame and second-guessing are practices of a prior life. Heaven will be wonderful, not because the streets are gold, but because our thoughts will be pure.

So what are you waiting on? Give God your best thoughts and see if he doesn't change your mind.

Next Door Savior

Set your mind on the things above,
not on the things that are on earth.

COLOSSIANS 3:2 NASB

Being always of good courage, and knowing that
while we are at home in the body we are absent
from the Lord—for we walk by faith, not by sight—we are
of good courage, I say, and prefer rather to be absent
from the body and to be at home with the Lord.

2 CORINTHIANS 5:6–8 NASB

But we all, with unveiled face,
beholding as in a mirror the glory of the Lord,
are being transformed into the same image from glory
to glory, just as from the Lord, the Spirit.

2 CORINTHIANS 3:18 NASB

*Are there any gods like you, L*ORD*?*
There are no gods like you.
You are wonderfully holy,
amazingly powerful,
a worker of miracles.

EXODUS 15:11 NCV

～

*Hope in the L*ORD*; for with the L*ORD *there is mercy,*
and with Him is abundant redemption.

PSALM 130:7

～

*Who among you fears the L*ORD*?*
Who obeys the voice of His Servant?
Who walks in darkness and has no light?
*Let him trust in the name of the L*ORD
and rely upon his God.

ISAIAH 50:10

Earthly seasons don't upset us. But unexpected personal ones certainly do. The way we panic at the sight of change, you'd think bombs were falling on Iowa.

"Run for your lives! Graduation is coming!"

"The board of directors just hired a new CEO. Take cover!"

"Load the women and children into the bus and head north. The department store is going out of business!"

Change trampolines our lives, and when it does, God sends someone special to stabilize us. Jesus gave his followers this promise: "When the Father sends the ... Holy Spirit—he will teach you everything. . . . I am leaving you with a gift—peace of mind and heart. . . . So don't be troubled or afraid" (John 14:26–27 NLT).

Fearless

Whoever loses his life for My sake will find it.

For fear of doing the wrong thing for God, some do nothing for God.

For fear of making the wrong kingdom decision, some make no kingdom decision.

For fear of messing up, some will miss out.

But you don't have to. Your God is a good God.

He lavished you with strengths in this life and a promise of the next. Go out on a limb; he won't let you fall. Take a big risk; he won't let you fail. He invites you to dream of the day you feel his hand on your shoulder and his eyes on your face. "Well done," he will say, "good and faithful servant."

Cure for the Common Life

*"His lord said to him,
'Well done, good and faithful servant;
you have been faithful over a few things,
I will make you ruler over many things.
Enter into the joy of your lord.'"*

MATTHEW 25:23

~~

*God is sheer mercy and grace;
not easily angered, he's rich in love.*

PSALM 103:8 MSG

It has become evident to the whole palace guard,
and to all the rest, that my chains are in Christ;
and most of the brethren in the Lord, having become
confident by my chains, are much more bold
to speak the word without fear.

PHILIPPIANS 1:13–14

[God] is the One who makes everything agree
with what he decides and wants.

EPHESIANS 1:11 NCV

The Lord will deliver me from every evil work
and preserve me for His heavenly kingdom.
To Him be glory forever and ever.

2 TIMOTHY 4:18

—❧—

The apostle Paul penned his final words in the bowels of a Roman prison, chained to a guard—within earshot of his executioner's footsteps. Worst-case scenario? Not from Paul's perspective. "God's looking after me, keeping me safe in the kingdom of heaven. All praise to him, praise forever!" (2 Timothy 4:18 MSG).

Paul chose to trust his Father.

Fearless

*Faith means being sure of the things we hope for
and knowing that something is real even if we do not see it.*

HEBREWS 11:1 NCV

*The righteous will...not be afraid of evil tidings;
his heart is steadfast, trusting in the LORD.*

PSALM 112:6–7

*We are surrounded by a great cloud of people
whose lives tell us what faith means.
So let us run the race that is before us
and never give up. We should remove from our lives
anything that would get in the way and the sin
that so easily holds us back.*

HEBREWS 12:1 NCV

Biographies of bold disciples begin with chapters of honest terror. Fear of death. Fear of failure. Fear of loneliness. Fear of a wasted life. Fear of failing to know God.

Faith begins when you see God on the mountain and you are in the valley and you know that you're too weak to make the climb. You see what you need . . . you see what you have . . . and what you have isn't enough to accomplish anything.

Moses had a sea in front and an enemy behind. The Israelites could swim or they could fight. But neither option was enough.

The Jerusalem church knew that they had no hope of getting Peter out of prison. They had Christians who would fight, but too few. They didn't need muscle. They needed a miracle.

Faith that begins with fear will end up nearer the Father.

In the Eye of the Storm

Nothing can ever separate us
from God's love. Neither death nor life,
neither angels nor demons, neither our fears for today
nor our worries about tomorrow—
not even the powers of hell
can separate us from God's love.

ROMANS 8:38 NLT

~

"Don't be afraid," [Jesus] said.
"Take courage. I am here!"

MATTHEW 14:27 NLT

He stirs up the sea with His mighty power, and by His understanding He breaks up the storm.

JOB 26:12

We expect Jesus to come in the form of peaceful hymns or Easter Sundays or quiet retreats. We expect to find him in morning devotionals, church suppers, and meditation. We never expect to see him in a bear market, pink slip, lawsuit, foreclosure, or war. We never expect to see him in a storm. But it is in storms that he does his finest work, for it is in storms that he has our keenest attention.

We cannot go where God is not. Look over your shoulder; that's God following you. Look into the storm; that's Christ coming toward you.

Fearless

"If anyone thirsts, let him come to Me and drink.
He who believes in Me, as the Scripture has said,
out of his heart will flow rivers of living water."

JOHN 7:37–38

As the deer pants for the water brooks,
So pants my soul for You, O God.
My soul thirsts for God, for the living God.

PSALM 42:1–2

I am the Alpha and the Omega,
the Beginning and the End.
I will give of the fountain of the water of life
freely to him who thirsts.

REVELATION 21:6

Your Maker wired you with thirst—a "low-fluid indicator." Let your fluid level grow low, and watch the signals flare. Dry mouth. Thick tongue. Deprive your body of necessary fluid, and your body will tell you.

Deprive your soul of spiritual water, and your soul will tell you. Dehydrated hearts send desperate messages. Snarling tempers. Waves of worry. Growling mastodons of guilt and fear. You think God wants you to live with these? Hopelessness. Sleeplessness. Irritability. Insecurity. These are symptoms of a dryness deep within.

Treat your soul as you treat your thirst. Flood your heart with a good swallow of water.

Where do you find water for the soul? Jesus gave an answer: "If anyone thirsts, let him come to Me and drink. He who believes in Me, as the Scripture has said, out of his heart will flow rivers of living water" (John 7:37–38).

Come Thirsty

Don't be afraid. Just have faith. . . .

LUKE 8:50 NLT

~

When the enemy comes in like a flood,
the Spirit of the LORD will lift up a standard against him.

ISAIAH 59:19

~

Don't be afraid. . . . Remember the Lord,
who is great and powerful. Fight for . . . your sons
and daughters, your wives, and your homes.

NEHEMIAH 4:14 NCV

We can take our parenting fears to Christ. In fact, if we don't, we'll take our fears out on our kids. Fear turns some parents into paranoid prison guards who monitor every minute, check the background of every friend. They stifle growth and communicate distrust. A family with no breathing room suffocates a child.

On the other hand, fear can also create permissive parents. For fear that their child will feel too confined or fenced in, they lower all boundaries. High on hugs and low on discipline. They don't realize that appropriate discipline is an expression of love. Permissive parents. Paranoid parents. How can we avoid the extremes? We pray.

Prayer is the saucer into which parental fears are poured to cool. Each time a parent prays, Christ responds. His big message to moms and dads? Bring your children to me. Raise them in a greenhouse of prayer.

Fearless

If You Are Afraid of Failure

Try hard to do right, and you will win friends; go looking for trouble, and you will find it. Trust in your wealth, and you will be a failure, but God's people will prosper like healthy plants.

PROVERBS 11:27–28 CEV

And everyone who has left houses or brothers or sisters or father or mother or children or lands, for my name's sake, will receive a hundredfold and will inherit eternal life.

MATTHEW 19:29 ESV

The Lord will guide you continually, giving you water when you are dry and restoring your strength. You will be like a well-watered garden, like an ever-flowing spring.

ISAIAH 58:11 NLT

"Therefore everyone who hears these words of mine and puts them into practice is like a wise man who built his house on the rock. The rain came down, the streams rose, and the winds blew and beat against that house; yet it did not fall, because it had its foundation on the rock."

MATTHEW 7:24–25 NIV

Too much activity gives you restless dreams;
too many words make you a fool.

ECCLESIASTES 5:3 NLT

Therefore do not cast away your confidence, which has great
reward. For you have need of endurance, so that after you
have done the will of God, you may receive the promise.

HEBREWS 10:35–36

And whatever you do, do it heartily, as to the Lord and not
to men, knowing that from the Lord you will receive the
reward of the inheritance; for you serve the Lord Christ.

COLOSSIANS 3:23–24

Each time [Jesus] said, "My grace is all you need. My power
works best in weakness." So now I am glad to boast about my
weaknesses, so that the power of Christ can work through me.

2 CORINTHIANS 12:9 NLT

Then Moses said to the LORD, "O my Lord, I am not
eloquent, neither before nor since You have spoken to Your
servant; but I am slow of speech and slow of tongue."
So the LORD said to him, "Who has made man's mouth?
Or who makes the mute, the deaf, the seeing, or the blind?
Have not I, the LORD? Now therefore, go, and I will be
with your mouth and teach you what you shall say."

EXODUS 4:10–12

The work of righteousness will be peace, and the effect of righteousness, quietness and assurance forever.

ISAIAH 32:17

But thanks be to God, who gives us the victory through our Lord Jesus Christ.

1 CORINTHIANS 15:57

But what things were gain to me, these I have counted loss for Christ. Yet indeed I also count all things loss for the excellence of the knowledge of Christ Jesus my Lord, for whom I have suffered the loss of all things, and count them as rubbish, that I may gain Christ and be found in Him.

PHILIPPIANS 3:7–9

I am God Most High! The only sacrifice I want is for you to be thankful and to keep your word. Pray to me in time of trouble. I will rescue you, and you will honor me.

PSALM 50:14–15 CEV

After these things the word of the LORD came to Abram in a vision, "Fear not, Abram, I am your shield; your reward shall be very great."

GENESIS 15:1 RSV

For [the man who fears the LORD] will never be upended; others will always remember one who is just. He does not fear bad news. He is confident; he trusts in the LORD. His resolve is firm; he will not succumb to fear before he looks in triumph on his enemies.

PSALM 112:6–8 NET

Do not work for the food which perishes, but for the food which endures to eternal life, which the Son of Man will give to you, for on Him the Father, God, has set His seal.

JOHN 6:27 NASB

Yet in all these things we are more than conquerors through Him who loved us.

ROMANS 8:37

We also glory in tribulations, knowing that tribulation produces perseverance; and perseverance, character; and character, hope. Now hope does not disappoint, because the love of God has been poured out in our hearts by the Holy Spirit who was given to us.

ROMANS 5:3–5

Only fear the LORD, and serve him faithfully with all your heart; for consider what great things he has done for you.

1 SAMUEL 12:24 NRSV

*And God is able to make all grace abound toward you,
that you, always having all sufficiency in all things,
may have an abundance for every good work.*

2 CORINTHIANS 9:8

*Our LORD and our God, you are my mighty rock, my
fortress, my protector. You are the rock where I am safe.
You are my shield, my powerful weapon, and my place
of shelter. You rescue me and keep me from being hurt.*

2 SAMUEL 22:2–3 CEV

*The Lord says, "If you love me and truly know who I am, I
will rescue you and keep you safe. When you are in trouble,
call out to me. I will answer and be there to protect and honor
you. You will live a long life and see my saving power."*

PSALM 91:14–16 CEV

*The Lord is my strength and my song;
he has become my salvation.*

PSALM 118:14 ESV

*So let us come boldly to the throne of our gracious
God. There we will receive his mercy, and we will
find grace to help us when we need it most.*

HEBREWS 4:16 NLT

"I am the vine; you are the branches. If you remain in me and I in you, you will bear much fruit; apart from me you can do nothing.

JOHN 15:5 NIV

Everyone has sinned and fallen short of God's glorious standard.

ROMANS 3:23 NCV

My dear children, I write this to you so that you will not sin. But if anybody does sin, we have an advocate with the Father—Jesus Christ, the Righteous One.

1 JOHN 2:1 NIV

"Woe to the rebellious children," says the LORD, "Who take counsel, but not of Me, and who devise plans, but not of My Spirit."

ISAIAH 30:1

The LORD will guide you continually, and satisfy your soul in drought, and strengthen your bones; you shall be like a watered garden, and like a spring of water, whose waters do not fail.

ISAIAH 58:11

Be strong and very courageous. Be careful to obey all the instructions Moses gave you. Do not deviate from them, turning either to the right or to the left. Then you will be successful in everything you do.

JOSHUA 1:7 NLT

*"For I know the plans I have for you," declares
the LORD, "plans to prosper you and not to harm
you, plans to give you hope and a future."*

JEREMIAH 29:11 NIV

The way of fools seems right to them, but the wise listen to advice.

PROVERBS 12:15 NIV

*Present your bodies a living sacrifice, holy, acceptable
to God, which is your reasonable service. And do not
be conformed to this world, but be transformed by the
renewing of your mind, that you may prove what is
that good and acceptable and perfect will of God.*

ROMANS 12:1–2

*Now to Him who is able to keep you from stumbling, and
to present you faultless before the presence of His glory with
exceeding joy, to God our Savior, who alone is wise, be glory and
majesty, dominion and power, both now and forever. Amen.*

JUDE VV. 24–25

FEAR NOT

God Is Never Surprised

Don't all of us live with a fear of the unknown? Don't all of us dread the horrible day when the thin curtain that separates us from evil might be pulled back and in we would tumble? Cancer. Murder. Rape. Death. How haunting is that gnawing awareness that we are not immune to life's mishaps and perils?

But God is not stumped by an evil world. He doesn't gasp in amazement at the depth of our faith or the depth of our failures. We can't surprise God with our cruelties. He knows the condition of the world . . . and loves it just the same. For just when we find a place where God would never be (like on a cross), we look again and there he is, in the flesh.

No Wonder They Call Him the Savior

———— ⚬❈⚬ ————

God is not the author of confusion but of peace,
as in all the churches of the saints.

1 CORINTHIANS 14:33

Our heart shall rejoice in Him,
because we have trusted in His holy name.

PSALM 33:21

Blessed be the LORD,
Who daily loads us with benefits.

PSALM 68:19

Leave all your worries with him,
because he cares for you.

1 PETER 5:7 GNT

～

Whatever you ask for in prayer,
believe that you have received it,
and it will be yours.

MARK 11:24 NIV

～

"If you remain in me and my words remain in you,
ask whatever you wish, and it will be given you."

JOHN 15:7 NIV

Don't pace up and down the floors of the waiting room; pray for a successful surgery.

Don't bemoan the collapse of an investment; ask God to help you.

Don't join the chorus of co-workers who complain about your boss; invite them to bow their heads with you and pray for him.

Inoculate yourself inwardly to face your fears outwardly. "Casting the whole of your care [all your anxieties, all your worries, all your concerns, once and for all] on Him." (1 Peter 5:7 AMP).

Fearless

He laid His right hand on me,
saying to me, "Do not be afraid; I am the First
and the Last. I am He who lives, and was dead,
and behold, I am alive forevermore."

REVELATION 1:17–18

We see Jesus, who was made a little lower than
the angels, now crowned with glory and honor
because he suffered death, so that by the grace of God
he might taste death for everyone.

HEBREWS 2:9 NIV

"O Death, where is your sting?
O Hades, where is your victory?"

1 CORINTHIANS 15:55

Someone you love dearly has been called into the unknown, and you are alone. Alone with your fears and alone with your doubts.

If God is God anywhere, he has to be God in the face of death. Pop psychology can deal with depression. Pep talks can deal with pessimism. Prosperity can handle hunger. But only God can deal with our ultimate dilemma—death. And only the God of the Bible has dared to stand on the canyon's edge and offer an answer: "I am the resurrection and the life. The one who believes in me will live, even though they die; and whoever lives by believing in me will never die" (John 11:25–26 NIV).

God Came Near

Whenever I am afraid,
I will trust in You.
In God (I will praise His word),
in God I have put my trust;
I will not fear.
What can flesh do to me?

PSALM 56:3–4

The LORD will give strength to His people;
the LORD will bless His people with peace.

PSALM 29:11

Why are you fearful, O you of little faith?"

MATTHEW 8:26

Imagine your life wholly untouched by angst.

What if faith, not fear, were your default reaction to threats? If you could hover a fear magnet over your heart and extract every last shaving of dread, insecurity, and doubt, what would remain?

Envision a day, just one day, absent the dread of failure, rejection, and calamity. Can you imagine a life with no fear? This is the possibility behind Jesus' question. "Why are you afraid?" he asks (Matthew 8:26 NCV).

Fearless

All your sons will be taught by the LORD, and great will be your children's peace. In righteousness you will be established: tyranny will be far from you; you will have nothing to fear.

ISAIAH 54:13–14 NIV

～

Pour out your heart like water
before the face of the Lord.
Lift your hands toward Him for the life
of your young children.

LAMENTATIONS 2:19

～

Jesus said, "Let the little children
come to Me, and do not forbid them;
for of such is the kingdom of heaven."

MATTHEW 19:14

Note to all panicking parents: Jesus heeds the concerns in parents' hearts.

After all, our kids were his kids first. "Don't you see that children are GOD's best gift? the fruit of the womb his generous legacy?" (Psalm 127:3 MSG). Before they were ours, they were his. Even as they are ours, they are still his.

We tend to forget this fact, regarding our children as "our" children, as though we have the final say in their health and welfare. We don't. All people are God's people, including the small people who sit at our tables. Wise are the parents who regularly give their children back to God.

Fearless

A man's heart plans his way,
*but the L*ORD *directs his steps.*

PROVERBS 16:9

∿

*A man's steps are of the L*ORD*;*
how then can a man understand his own way?

PROVERBS 20:24

∿

*The L*ORD *will guide you continually,*
and satisfy your soul in drought.

ISAIAH 58:11

"This is the day the LORD has made; we will rejoice and be glad in it" (Psalm 118:24).

"This is the day" includes every day. Divorce days, final-exam days, surgery days, tax days. Sending-your-firstborn-off-to-college days.

God made this day, ordained this hard hour, designed the details of this wrenching moment. He isn't on holiday. He still holds the conductor's baton, sits in the cockpit, and occupies the universe's only throne. Each day emerges from God's drawing room. Including this one.

Every Day Deserves a Chance

Don't be afraid!
Stand still and you
*will see the L*ORD
save you today.

EXODUS 14:13 NCV

Fear will always knock on your door. Just don't invite it in for dinner, and for heaven's sake don't offer it a bed for the night. Let's embolden our hearts with a select number of Jesus' "do not fear" statements. Fear may fill our world, but it doesn't have to fill our hearts. The promise of Christ [is] simple: we can fear less tomorrow than we do today.

Fearless

The true children of God are those
who let God's Spirit lead them. The Spirit we received
does not make us slaves again to fear; it makes us children of
God. With that Spirit we cry out, "Father."

ROMANS 8:14–15 NCV

~

Be strong, and let us show ourselves courageous
for the sake of our people and for the cities of our God;
and may the LORD do what is good in His sight.

2 SAMUEL 10:12 NASB

*[Simon Peter] and all who were with him
were astonished at the catch of fish which they had taken. . . .
And Jesus said to Simon,
"Do not be afraid. From now on you will catch men."*

LUKE 5:9–10

*"I am the LORD your God,
who divided the sea whose waves roared—
the LORD of hosts is His name. . . .
I have covered you with the shadow of My hand."*

ISAIAH 51:15–16

*I create the light and make the darkness.
I send good times and bad times.
I, the LORD, am the one who does these things.*

ISAIAH 45:7 NLT

The financial aid office says, "No."

A doctor says, "Pregnant."

The boss says, "Transfer."

Change always brings fear before it brings faith.
We always assume the worst before we look for the best.
God interrupts our lives with something we've never
seen, and rather than praise, we panic! We interpret the
presence of a problem as the absence of God.

We forget that he says: "I create the light and make the
darkness. I send good times and bad times. I, the LORD,
am the one who does these things" (Isaiah 45:7 NLT).

God Came Near

Trust in him at all times, O people;
pour out your hearts to him,
for God is our refuge.

PSALM 62:8 NIV

~

The LORD is my rock, my fortress and my deliverer;
my God is my rock, in whom I take refuge,
my shield and the horn of my salvation.
He is my stronghold, my refuge and my savior.

2 SAMUEL 22:2–3 NIV

~

We also have joy with our troubles,
because we know that these troubles produce patience.
And patience produces character, and character produces hope.
And this hope will never disappoint us, because God has poured
out his love to fill our hearts.

ROMANS 5:3–5 NCV

You move down the ladder, out of the house, over for the new guy, up through the system. All this moving. Some changes welcome, others not. And in those rare seasons when you think the world has settled down, watch out. One seventy-seven-year-old recently told a friend of mine, "I've had a good life. I am enjoying my life now, and I am looking forward to the future." Two weeks later a tornado ripped through the region, taking the lives of his son, daughter-in-law, grandson, and daughter-in-law's mother. We just don't know, do we? On our list of fears, the fear of what's next demands a prominent position. We might request a decaffeinated life, but we don't get it.

What person passes through life surprise free? If you don't want change, go to a soda machine; that's the only place you won't find any.

Fearless

In the time of trouble He shall hide me in His pavilion;
in the secret place of His tabernacle He shall hide me.

PSALM 27:5

Jesus Christ is the same yesterday, today, and forever.

HEBREWS 13:8 NLT

His divine power has given to us
all things that pertain to life and godliness.

2 PETER 1:3

God gets into things! Red Seas. Big fish. Lions' dens and furnaces. Bankrupt businesses and jail cells. Judean wildernesses, weddings, funerals, and Galilean tempests. Look and you'll find what everyone from Moses to Martha discovered: God in the middle of our storms.

That includes yours.

Next Door Savior

*Remember that I commanded you
to be strong and brave. Don't be afraid,
because the L*ORD *your God will be with you
everywhere you go.*

JOSHUA 1:9 NCV

~

*Search me, O God, and know my heart;
try me, and know my anxieties;
and see if there is any wicked way in me,
and lead me in the way everlasting.*

PSALM 139:23–24

Ask and it will be given to you; seek and you will find; knock and the door will be opened to you.

LUKE 11:9 NIV

Become a worry-slapper. Treat frets like mosquitoes. The moment a concern surfaces, deal with it. Don't dwell on it. Head off worries before they get the best of you.

Don't waste an hour wondering what your boss thinks; ask her.

Before you diagnose that mole as cancer, have it examined.

Instead of assuming you'll never get out of debt, consult an expert.

Be a doer, not a stewer.

Fearless

He gives strength to those who are tired
and more power to those who are weak.
But the people who trust the LORD will become strong again.
They will rise up as an eagle in the sky;
they will run and not need rest;
they will walk and not become tired.

ISAIAH 40:29, 31 NCV

~~

He had to enter into every detail of human life.
Then, when he came before God as high priest to get rid
of the people's sins, he would have already experienced it all
himself—all the pain, all the testing—and would
be able to help where help was needed.

HEBREWS 2:17–18 MSG

~~

Though He was a Son, yet He learned obedience
by the things which He suffered. And having been
perfected, He became the author of eternal salvation
to all who obey Him.

HEBREWS 5:8–9

Jesus has been there. He experienced "all the pain, all the testing" (Hebrews 2:18 MSG). Jesus was angry enough to purge the temple, hungry enough to eat raw grain, distraught enough to weep in public, fun loving enough to be called a drunkard, winsome enough to attract kids, weary enough to sleep in a storm-bounced boat, poor enough to sleep on dirt and borrow a coin for a sermon illustration, radical enough to get kicked out of town, responsible enough to care for his mother, tempted enough to know the smell of Satan, and fearful enough to sweat blood.

But why? Why would heaven's finest Son endure earth's toughest pain? So you would know that "he is able . . . to run to the cry of . . . those who are being tempted and tested and tried" (Hebrews 2:18 AMP).

Whatever you are facing, he knows how you feel.

Next Door Savior

You will not have to fight this battle. Take up your positions; stand firm and see the deliverance the LORD will give you.

2 CHRONICLES 20:17

NIV

Our problems have always been God's possibilities.

The kidnapping of Joseph resulted in the preservation of his family.

The persecution of Daniel led to a cabinet position.

Christ entered the world by a surprise pregnancy and redeemed it through his unjust murder.

Dare we believe what the Bible teaches? That no disaster is ultimately fatal?

Fearless

[The angel] said to me, "Do not fear, Daniel,
for from the first day that you set your heart
to understand, and to humble yourself before your God, your
words were heard; and I have come
because of your words."

DANIEL 10:12

∼

When the servant of the man of God
arose early and went out, there was an army,
surrounding the city with horses and chariots.
And his servant said to him, "Alas, my master!
What shall we do?" So he answered, "Do not fear,
for those who are with us are more than those
who are with them."

2 KINGS 6:15–16

*Let the beauty of the L*ORD *our God*
be upon us, and establish the work of our hands
for us; yes, establish the work of our hands.

PSALM 90:17

*I will sing to the L*ORD *as long as I live;*
I will sing praise to my God while I have my being.
May my meditation be sweet to Him;
*I will be glad in the L*ORD.

PSALM 104:33–34

*What shall I render to the L*ORD
for all His benefits toward me?
I will take up the cup of salvation,
*and call upon the name of the L*ORD.

PSALM 116:12–13

Eternal instants. You've had them. We all have.

Sharing a porch swing on a summer evening with your grandchild.

Putting your arm into your husband's as you stroll through the golden leaves and breathe the brisk autumn air.

Listening to your six-year-old thank God for everything from goldfish to Grandma.

Such moments are necessary because they remind us that everything is okay. The King is still on the throne and life is still worth living. Eternal instants remind us that love is still the greatest possession and the future is nothing to fear.

God Came Near

We know that all things work together
for good to those who love God, to those
who are the called according to His purpose.

ROMANS 8:28

～

He who is mighty has done great things for me,
and holy is His name.

LUKE 1:49

～

"I have good plans for you, not plans to hurt you.
I will give you hope and a good future.
Then you will call my name.
You will come to me and pray to me, and I
will listen to you. You will search for me. And when you
search for me with all your heart, you will find me!"

JEREMIAH 29:11–13 NCV

I have a friend who was dreading a letter from the IRS. According to their early calculation, he owed them money, money he did not have. He was told to expect a letter detailing the amount. When the letter arrived, his courage failed him. He couldn't bear to open it, so the envelope sat on his desk for five days while he writhed in dread. How much could it be? Where would he get the funds? For how long would he be sent to prison? Finally he summoned the gumption to open the envelope. He found, not a bill to be paid, but a check to be cashed. The IRS, as it turned out, owed him money! He had wasted five days on needless fear.

Why assume the worst? As followers of God, you and I have a huge asset. We know everything is going to turn out all right. Christ hasn't budged from his throne, and Romans 8:28 hasn't evaporated from the Bible.

Fearless

You will hear of wars and rumors of wars,
but see to it that you are not alarmed.

MATTHEW 24:6 NIV

God has not given us a spirit of fear, but of power
and of love and of a sound mind.

2 TIMOTHY 1:7

When you lie down, you will not be afraid;
yes, you will lie down and your sleep will be sweet.

PROVERBS 3:24

A dose of fright can keep a child from running across a busy road or an adult from smoking a pack of cigarettes. Fear is the appropriate reaction to a burning building or growling dog. Fear itself is not a sin. But it can lead to sin.

If we medicate fear with angry outbursts, drinking binges, sullen withdrawals, self-starvation, or viselike control, we exclude God from the solution and exacerbate the problem. We subject ourselves to a position of fear, allowing anxiety to dominate and define our lives. Joy-sapping worries. Day-numbing dread. Repeated bouts of insecurity that petrify and paralyze us.

Hysteria is not from God.

Fearless

If You Are Afraid
of the Unknown

"You will hear of wars and rumors of wars, but
see to it that you are not alarmed. Such things
must happen, but the end is still to come."

MATTHEW 24:6 NIV

When the earth quakes and its people live in turmoil,
I am the one who keeps its foundations firm.

PSALM 75:3 NLT

For godly grief and the pain God is permitted to direct,
produce a repentance that leads and contributes to salvation
and deliverance from evil, and it never brings regret; but
worldly grief (the hopeless sorrow that is characteristic of the
pagan world) is deadly [breeding and ending in death].

2 CORINTHIANS 7:10 AMP

"For I have given rest to the weary and joy to the sorrowing."

JEREMIAH 31:25 NLT

Do not be wise in your own eyes; fear the LORD and turn away from evil. It will be healing to your body and refreshment to your bones. Honor the LORD from your wealth and from the first of all your produce; so your barns will be filled with plenty and your vats will overflow with new wine.

PROVERBS 3:7–10 NASB

Cry aloud before the Lord, O walls of beautiful Jerusalem! Let your tears flow like a river day and night. Give yourselves no rest; give your eyes no relief.

LAMENTATIONS 2:18 NLT

May our Lord Jesus Christ himself and God our Father, who loved us and by his grace gave us eternal encouragement and good hope, encourage your hearts and strengthen you in every good deed and word.

2 THESSALONIANS 2:16–17 NIV

Because of the tender mercy of our God, by which the rising sun will come to us from heaven to shine on those living in darkness and in the shadow of death, to guide our feet into the path of peace.

LUKE 1:78–79 NIV

"So do not worry about tomorrow; for tomorrow will care for itself. Each day has enough trouble of its own."

MATTHEW 6:34 NASB

*He shall cover you with His feathers, and under His wings
you shall take refuge; His truth shall be your shield and
buckler. You shall not be afraid of the terror by night, nor of
the arrow that flies by day, nor of the pestilence that walks in
darkness, nor of the destruction that lays waste at noonday.*

PSALM 91:4–6

*The high and lofty one who lives in eternity, the Holy One, says
this: "I live in the high and holy place with those whose spirits
are contrite and humble. I restore the crushed spirit of the
humble and revive the courage of those with repentant hearts.*

ISAIAH 57:15 NLT

*When he heard this, Jesus said, "This sickness will
not end in death. No, it is for God's glory so that
God's Son may be glorified through it."*

JOHN 11:4 NIV

*Then you will walk safely in your way,
and your foot will not stumble.
When you lie down, you will not be afraid; yes, you
will lie down and your sleep will be sweet.
Do not be afraid of sudden terror, Nor of
trouble from the wicked when it comes.*

PROVERBS 3:23–25

*I sought the Lord, and He heard me, and
delivered me from all my fears.*

PSALM 34:4

*Behold, God is my salvation, I will trust and not be afraid; "For Yah,
the Lord, is my strength and song; He also has become my salvation."*

ISAIAH 12:2

*He will be your safety. He is full of salvation, wisdom, and
knowledge. Respect for the Lord is the greatest treasure.*

ISAIAH 33:6 NCV

*But I trust in your unfailing love; my heart rejoices in your salvation.
I will sing the Lord's praise, for he has been good to me.*

PSALM 13:5–6 NIV

*While he was still speaking, behold, a bright cloud overshadowed
them; and suddenly a voice came out of the cloud, saying, "This is My
beloved Son, in whom I am well pleased. Hear Him!" And when the
disciples heard it, they fell on their faces and were greatly afraid. But
Jesus came and touched them and said, "Arise, and do not be afraid."*

MATTHEW 17:5–7

*For God has not given us a spirit of fear, but of
power and of love and of a sound mind.*

2 TIMOTHY 1:7

*When his people pray for help, he listens and rescues them
from their troubles. The LORD is there to rescue all who are
discouraged and have given up hope. The LORD's people may
suffer a lot, but he will always bring them safely through.*

PSALM 34:17–19 CEV

*Trust in the LORD with all your heart, and lean
not on your own understanding; in all your ways
acknowledge Him, and He shall direct your paths.*

PROVERBS 3:5–6

*And coming to Him as to a living stone which has been
rejected by men, but is choice and precious in the sight
of God, you also, as living stones, are being built up as a
spiritual house for a holy priesthood, to offer up spiritual
sacrifices acceptable to God through Jesus Christ.*

1 PETER 2:4–5 NASB

*Peace I leave with you; my peace I give you. I do
not give to you as the world gives. Do not let your
hearts be troubled and do not be afraid.*

JOHN 14:27 NIV

*I will instruct you and teach you in the way you
should go; I will guide you with My eye.*

PSALM 32:8

Are you hurting? Pray. Do you feel great? Sing. Are you sick? Call the church leaders together to pray and anoint you with oil in the name of the Master. Believing-prayer will heal you, and Jesus will put you on your feet. And if you've sinned, you'll be forgiven—healed inside and out.

JAMES 5:13–15 MSG

Fear of the Lord is the foundation of true knowledge, but fools despise wisdom and discipline.

PROVERBS 1:7 NLT

As for me, I call to God, and the Lord saves me. Evening, morning and noon I cry out in distress, and he hears my voice. He rescues me unharmed from the battle waged against me, even though many oppose me. God, who is enthroned from of old, who does not change—he will hear them and humble them because they have no fear of God.

PSALM 55:16–19 NIV

You will not be harmed, though thousands fall all around you. And with your own eyes you will see the punishment of the wicked. The Lord Most High is your fortress. Run to him for safety, and no terrible disasters will strike you or your home.

PSALM 91:7–10 CEV

If any of you lacks wisdom, let him ask of God, who gives to all liberally and without reproach, and it will be given to him.

JAMES 1:5

Now this is the confidence that we have in Him, that if we ask anything according to His will, He hears us. And if we know that He hears us, whatever we ask, we know that we have the petitions that we have asked of Him.

1 JOHN 5:14–15

Oh, give thanks to the LORD, for He is good! For His mercy endures forever. . . . Let those who fear the LORD now say, "His mercy endures forever." I called on the LORD in distress; the LORD answered me and set me in a broad place.

PSALM 118:1, 4–5

When Jesus spoke again to the people, he said, "I am the light of the world. Whoever follows me will never walk in darkness, but will have the light of life."

JOHN 8:12 NIV

I will instruct you and teach you in the way you should go; I will guide you with My eye.

PSALM 32:8

You make known to me the path of life; you will fill me with joy in your presence, with eternal pleasures at your right hand.

PSALM 16:11 NIV

FEAR NOT

God Provides and Guides

God is the great giver. The great provider. The fount of every blessing. Absolutely generous and utterly dependable.

The resounding and recurring message of Scripture is clear: God owns it all. God shares it all.

Trust him, not stuff!

Move from the fear of scarcity to the comfort of provision. Less hoarding, more sharing. "Do good . . . be rich in good works, ready to give, willing to share" (1 Timothy 6:18).

And, most of all, replace fear of the coming winter with faith in the living God.

Fearless

———— ⌘ ————

*Do not worry about tomorrow, for tomorrow
will worry about its own things. Sufficient for the day
is its own trouble.*

MATTHEW 6:34

*Command those who are rich in this present age not to be
haughty, nor to trust in uncertain riches but in the living God,
who gives us richly all things to enjoy.*

1 TIMOTHY 6:17

*Yours, O LORD, is the greatness and the power
and the glory and the majesty and the splendor,
for everything in heaven and earth is yours.*

1 CHRONICLES 29:11 NIV

*I sought the L*ORD*, and He heard me,*
and delivered me from all my fears.

PSALM 34:4

~

*Blessed is that man who makes the L*ORD *his trust.*

PSALM 40:4

~

*"I, the L*ORD *your God, will hold your right hand,*
saying to you, 'Fear not, I will help you.'"

ISAIAH 41:13

He doesn't want your money. He doesn't want your diamonds. He won't go after your car. He wants something far more precious. He wants your peace of mind—your joy.

His name?

Fear.

His task is to take your courage and leave you timid and trembling. His modus operandi is to manipulate you with the mysterious, to taunt you with the unknown. Fear of death, fear of failure, fear of God, fear of tomorrow—his arsenal is vast. His goal? To create cowardly, joyless souls.

The Applause of Heaven

*The righteous shall be glad in the L*ORD*, and trust in Him.*
and all the upright in heart shall glory.

PSALM 64:10

*Blessed is the man who trusts in the L*ORD*,*
*and whose hope is the L*ORD*.*
For he shall be like a tree planted by the waters,
which spreads out its roots by the river,
and will not fear when heat comes;
but its leaf will be green,
and will not be anxious in the year of drought,
nor will cease from yielding fruit.

JEREMIAH 17:7–8

*The L*ORD *is my strength and my shield;*
my heart trusted in Him, and I am helped;
therefore my heart greatly rejoices,
and with my song I will praise Him.

PSALM 28:7

There's a stampede of fear out there. Let's not get caught in it. Let's be among those who stay calm. Let's recognize danger but not be overwhelmed. Acknowledge threats but refuse to be defined by them. Let others breathe the polluted air of anxiety, not us. Let's be numbered among those who hear a different voice, God's.

Enough of these shouts of despair, wails of doom. Why pay heed to the doomsdayer on Wall Street or the purveyor of gloom in the newspaper? We will incline our ears elsewhere: upward. We will turn to our Maker, and because we do, we will fear less.

Fearless

The LORD is good to those who wait for Him,
to the soul who seeks Him.
It is good that one should hope and wait quietly
for the salvation of the LORD.

LAMENTATIONS 3:25–26

〰

I will instruct you and teach you in the way you should go;
I will guide you with My eye.

PSALM 32:8

〰

My mouth shall speak wisdom,
and the meditation of my heart
shall give understanding.

PSALM 49:3

"Go confidently to the throne of God's kindness to receive mercy and find kindness, which will help us *at the right time*" (Hebrews 4:16 GOD'S WORD, emphasis mine).

You don't have wisdom for tomorrow's problems. But you will tomorrow.

You don't have resources for tomorrow's needs. But you will tomorrow.

You don't have courage for tomorrow's challenges. But you will when tomorrow comes.

God meets daily needs daily and miraculously.

Every Day Deserves a Chance

"Do not fear, nor be afraid;
have I not told you from that time, and declared it?
You are My witnesses.
Is there a God besides Me?
Indeed there is no other Rock;
I know not one."

ISAIAH 44:8

~

You will hear of wars and rumors of wars,
but see to it that you are not alarmed.
Such things must happen, but the end is still to come.

MATTHEW 24:6 NIV

The LORD is good,
a stronghold in the
day of trouble; and
He knows those who
trust in Him.

NAHUM 1:7

Life is a dangerous endeavor. We pass our days in the shadows of ominous realities. The power to annihilate humanity has, it seems, been placed in the hands of people who are happy to do so. If the global temperature rises a few more degrees . . . if classified information falls into sinister hands . . . if the wrong person pushes the wrong red button. . . . What if things only get worse?

Christ tells us that they will. He predicts spiritual bailouts, ecological turmoil, and worldwide persecution. Yet in the midst of it all, he contends bravery is still an option.

Fearless

Whatever you do in word or deed,
do all in the name of the Lord Jesus,
giving thanks to God the Father through Him.

COLOSSIANS 3:17

Strengthen yourselves so that you will live
here on earth doing what God wants,
not the evil things people want.

1 PETER 4:2 NCV

Our offering to God is this:
We are the sweet smell of Christ
among those who are being saved
and among those who are being lost.

2 CORINTHIANS 2:15 NCV

"As the Spirit of the Lord works within us, we become more and more like him" (2 Corinthians 3:18 TLB).

Can you think of a greater gift than to be like Jesus?

Christ felt no guilt; God wants to banish yours.

Jesus had no bad habits: God wants to remove yours.

Jesus had no fear of death; God wants you to be fearless.

Jesus had kindness for the diseased and mercy for the rebellious and courage for the challenges. God wants you to have the same. He wants you to be just like Jesus.

Just Like Jesus

The Helper, the Holy Spirit,
whom the Father will send in My name,
He will teach you all things, and bring
to your remembrance all things that I said to you.

JOHN 14:26

～

"Fear not, for I have redeemed you;
I have called you by your name
you are Mine."

ISAIAH 43:1

～

As many as are led by the Spirit of God,
these are sons of God. For you did not receive the spirit
of bondage again to fear, but you received the Spirit of adoption
by whom we cry out, "Abba, Father."

ROMANS 8:14–15

You will never face the future without God's help. You have a travel companion.

When you place your faith in Christ, Christ places his Spirit before, behind, and within you. Not a strange spirit, but the *same* Spirit: the *parakletos*. As Jesus sends you into new seasons, he sends his counselor to go with you.

God never sends you out alone. Are you on the eve of change? Do you find yourself looking into a new chapter? Is the foliage of your world showing signs of a new season? Heaven's message for you is clear: when everything else changes, God's presence never does. You journey in the company of the Holy Spirit.

Fearless

Whatever you ask in My name,
that I will do, that the Father
may be glorified in the Son.

JOHN 14:13

"If you have faith as a mustard seed . . . nothing
will be impossible for you."

MATTHEW 17:20

He raises the poor out of the dust,
and lifts the needy out of the ash heap.

PSALM 113:7

"If God is for us, who can be against us?"(Romans 8:31 NIV). The question is not simply, "Who can be against us?" You could answer that one. Who is against you? Disease, inflation, corruption, exhaustion. Calamities confront, and fears imprison. Were Paul's question, "Who can be against us?" we could list our foes much easier than we could fight them. But that is not the question. The question is, *IF GOD IS FOR US, who can be against us?*

God is for you. Your parents may have forgotten you, your teachers may have neglected you, your siblings may be ashamed of you; but within reach of your prayers is the maker of the oceans. God!

In the Grip of Grace

You drew near on the day I called on You,
and said, "Do not fear!"

LAMENTATIONS 3:57

Watch and pray so that you will not fall into temptation.
The spirit is willing, but the flesh is weak.

MARK 14:38 NIV

Come to Me, all you who labor and are heavy laden,
and I will give you rest.

MATTHEW 11:28

Amidst the olive trees [in Gethsemane's garden,] Jesus "fell to the ground. He prayed that, if it were possible, the awful hour awaiting him might pass him by. 'Abba, Father,' he cried out, 'everything is possible for you. Please take this cup of suffering away from me. Yet I want your will to be done, not mine'" (Mark 14:35–36 NLT).

The cup equaled Jesus' worst-case scenario: to be the recipient of God's wrath. He had never felt God's fury; he didn't deserve to. He'd never experienced isolation from his Father; the two had been one for eternity. He'd never known physical death; he was an immortal being. Yet within a few short hours, Jesus would face them all. And Jesus was afraid. Deathly afraid. And what he did with his fear shows us what to do with ours.

He prayed. Jesus faced his ultimate fear with honest prayer.

Fearless

The same day at evening, being the first day of the week, when the doors were shut where the disciples were assembled, for fear of the Jews, Jesus came and stood in the midst, and said to them, "Peace be with you."

JOHN 20:19

~

When they had prayed, the place where they were assembled together was shaken; and they were all filled with the Holy Spirit, and they spoke the word of God with boldness.

ACTS 4:31

~

They stayed there a long time, speaking boldly in the Lord, who was bearing witness to the word of His grace, granting signs and wonders to be done by their hands.

ACTS 14:3

Remember the fear of Christ's followers at the Crucifixion? They ran. Scared as cats in a dog pound.

But fast-forward forty days. Bankrupt traitors have become a force of life-changing fury. Peter is preaching in the very precinct where Christ was arrested. Followers of Christ defy the enemies of Christ. Whip them and they'll worship. Lock them up and they'll launch a jailhouse ministry. As bold after the Resurrection as they were cowardly before it.

Explanation:

Greed? They made no money.

Power? They gave all the credit to Christ.

Popularity? Most were killed for their beliefs.

Only one explanation remains—a resurrected Christ and his Holy Spirit.

Next Door Savior

"*I, even I, am He who comforts you.*
Who are you that you should be afraid . . . ?"

ISAIAH 51:12

~

The LORD *is my light and the one who saves me.*
So why should I fear anyone? The LORD *protects my life.*
So why should I be afraid?

PSALM 27:1 NCV

~

Look at the birds. They don't plant or harvest
or store food in barns, for your heavenly Father feeds them. And
aren't you far more valuable to him than they are? Can all your
worries add a single moment to your life?

MATTHEW 6:26–27 NLT

Shortfalls and depletions inhabit our trails. Not enough time, luck, wisdom, intelligence. We are running out of everything, it seems, and so we worry. But worry doesn't work.

Fret won't fill a bird's belly with food or a flower's petal with color.

Birds and flowers seem to get along just fine, and they don't take antacids.

What's more, you can dedicate a decade of anxious thoughts to the brevity of life and not extend it by one minute. Worry accomplishes nothing.

Fearless

I am the living bread which came down
from heaven. If anyone eats of this bread,
he will live forever; and the bread that I shall give
is My flesh, which I shall give for the life of the world.

JOHN 6:51

~

"I am the good shepherd. The good shepherd
gives His life for the sheep."

JOHN 10:11

~

Jesus said to him, "I am the way, the truth, and the life.
No one comes to the Father except through Me."

JOHN 14:6

The disciples were alone in the storm for nine tempestuous hours! Long enough for more than one disciple to ask, "Where is Jesus? He knows we are in the boat. For heaven's sake, it was his idea. Is God anywhere near?"

And from within the storm comes an unmistakable voice: "Courage! I am! Don't be afraid!" (Matthew 14:27, literal translation).

From the center of the storm, the unwavering Jesus shouts, "I am." Tall in the Twin Towers wreckage. Bold against the Galilean waves. ICU, battlefield, boardroom, prison cell, or maternity ward—whatever your storm, "I am."

Christ comes astride the waves and declares the words engraved on every wise heart: "Courage! I am! Don't be afraid!"

Next Door Savior

> *Cast your*
> *burden on the LORD,*
> *and He shall*
> *sustain you.*
>
> PSALM 55:22

I wonder, how many burdens is Jesus carrying for us that we know nothing about? We're aware of some. He carries our sin. He carries our shame. He carries our eternal debt. But are there others? Has he lifted fears before we felt them? Has he carried our confusion so we wouldn't have to? Those times when we have been surprised by our own sense of peace? Could it be that Jesus has lifted our anxiety onto his shoulders and placed a yoke of kindness on ours?

And how often do we thank him for his kindness? Not often enough. But does our ingratitude restrict his kindness? No. "Because he is kind even to people who are ungrateful and full of sin" (Luke 6:35 NCV).

A Love Worth Giving

He gathers the lambs
in his arms and carries them
close to his heart.

ISAIAH 40:11 NIV

~

The eyes of the LORD are on the righteous,
and His ears are open to their prayers.

1 PETER 3:12

God is our protection and our strength.
He always helps in times of trouble.
So we will not be afraid even if the earth shakes,
or the mountains fall into the sea.

PSALM 46:1–2 NCV

The steadfast love of the LORD never ceases,
his mercies never come to an end; they are new every morning;
great is thy faithfulness.

LAMENTATIONS 3:22–23 RSV

Wait for the LORD; be strong and let your heart
take courage; yes, wait for the LORD.

PSALM 27:14 NASB

God's call to courage is not a call to naïveté or ignorance. We aren't to be oblivious to the overwhelming challenges that life brings. We're to counterbalance them with long looks at God's accomplishments. "We must *pay much closer attention* to what we have heard, so that we do not drift away from it" (Hebrews 2:1 NASB, emphasis mine). Do whatever it takes to keep your gaze on Jesus.

When a friend of mine spent several days in the hospital at the bedside of her husband, she relied on hymns to keep her spirits up. Every few minutes she stepped into the restroom and sang a few verses of "Great Is Thy Faithfulness." Do likewise! Memorize scripture. Read biographies of great lives. Ponder the testimonies of faithful Christians. Make the deliberate decision to set your hope on [Jesus]. Courage is always a possibility.

Fearless

You are my strong refuge.
Let my mouth be filled with Your praise
and with Your glory all the day.

PSALM 71:7–8

∿

Blessed is the man whom You instruct, O LORD,
and teach out of Your law.

PSALM 94:12

∿

Christ also suffered for us, leaving us an example,
that you should follow His steps: "Who committed no sin, nor
was deceit found in His mouth"; who, when He was reviled, did
not revile in return; when He suffered,
He did not threaten, but committed Himself to Him
who judges righteously.

1 PETER 2:21—23

Millions who face the chill of empty pockets or the fears of sudden change turn to Christ. Why?

Because he's been there.

He's been to Nazareth, where he made deadlines and paid bills; to Galilee, where he recruited direct reports and separated fighters; to Jerusalem, where he stared down critics and stood up against cynics.

We have our Nazareths as well, demands and due dates. Jesus wasn't the last to build a team; accusers didn't disappear with Jerusalem's temple. Why seek Jesus's help with your challenges? Because he's been there.

3:16: The Numbers of Hope

Everything comes from God alone.
Everything lives by his power,
and everything is for his glory.

ROMANS 11:36 TLB

~

Take in with all followers of Jesus
the extravagant dimensions of Christ's love.
Reach out and experience the breadth! Test its length! Plumb
the depths! Rise to the heights! Live full lives,
full in the fullness of God.

EPHESIANS 3:18-19 MSG

~

I'll write the book on your righteousness,
talk up your salvation the livelong day,
never run out of good things to write or say.

PSALM 71:15 MSG

Jesus performed two bread-multiplying miracles: in one he fed 5,000 people, in the other 4,000. Still his disciples, who witnessed both feasts, worried about empty pantries. A frustrated Jesus rebuked them: "Are your hearts too hard to take it in? . . . Don't you remember anything at all?" (Mark 8:17–18 NLT).

Short memories harden the heart. Make careful note of God's blessings. Declare with David: "[I will] daily add praise to praise. I'll write the book on your righteousness, talk up your salvation the livelong day, never run out of good things to write or say" (Psalm 71:14–15 MSG).

Catalog God's goodnesses. Meditate on them. He has fed you, led you, and earned your trust. Remember what God has done for you.

3:16: The Numbers of Hope

The LORD is my shepherd;
I shall not want.
He makes me to lie down in green pastures;
He leads me beside the still waters.

PSALM 23:1–2

You will keep him in perfect peace,
whose mind is stayed on You.

ISAIAH 26:3

Take My yoke upon you and learn from Me,
for I am gentle and lowly in heart,
and you will find rest for your souls.

MATTHEW 11:29

For you to be healthy, you must rest. Slow down, and God will heal you. He will bring rest to your mind, to your body, and most of all to your soul. He will lead you to green pastures. "He makes me to lie down in green pastures" (Psalm 23:2).

Green pastures were not the natural terrain of Judea. Even today they are white and parched. Any green pasture in Judea is the work of some shepherd. He has cleared the rough, rocky land. Stumps have been torn out, and brush has been burned. Irrigation. Cultivation. Such are the works of a shepherd.

With his own pierced hands, Jesus created a pasture for the soul. He tore out the thorny underbrush of condemnation. He pried loose the huge boulders of sin. In their place he planted seeds of grace and dug ponds of mercy.

And he invites us to rest there.

Traveling Light

"Do not fear, little flock, for it is your Father's
good pleasure to give you the kingdom."

LUKE 12:32

~

Thus says the LORD, your Redeemer,
and He who formed you from the womb:
"I am the LORD, who makes all things,
Who stretches out the heavens all alone,
Who spreads abroad the earth by Myself."

ISAIAH 44:24

~

To the LORD your God belong the heavens,
even the highest heavens, the earth and everything in it.

DEUTERONOMY 10:14 NIV

When homes foreclose or pensions evaporate, we need a shepherd. In Christ we have one. And his "good pleasure [is] to give you the kingdom" (Luke 12:32). Giving characterizes God's creation. From the first page of Scripture, he is presented as a philanthropic creator. He produces in pluralities: stars, plants, birds, and animals. Every gift arrives in bulk, multiples, and medleys.

Scrooge didn't create the world; God did.

Psalm 104 celebrates this lavish creation with twenty-three verses of itemized blessings: the heavens and the earth, the waters and streams and trees and birds and goats and wine and oil and bread and people and lions. God is the source of "innumerable teeming things, living things both small and great. . . . These all wait for You, that You may give them their food in due season" (vv. 25, 27).

And he does.

Fearless

Looking unto Jesus, the author and finisher
of our faith, who for the joy that was set before Him
endured the cross, despising the shame, and has sat down at the
right hand of the throne of God.

HEBREWS 12:2

～

Let us come boldly to the throne
of our gracious God. There we will receive
his mercy, and we will find grace to help us
when we need it most.

HEBREWS 4:16 NLT

Your word is a lamp to my feet and a light to my path.

PSALM 119:105

God isn't going to let you see the distant scene. So you might as well quit looking for it. He promises a lamp unto our feet, not a crystal ball into the future (Psalm 119:105). We do not need to know what will happen tomorrow. We only need to know he leads us and "we will find grace to help us when we need it" (Hebrews 4:16 NLT).

God meets daily needs daily. Not weekly or annually. He will give you what you need when it is needed.

Traveling Light

If You Are Afraid of Financial Difficulties

And the Lord appeared to him the same night and said, "I am the God of Abraham your father; fear not, for I am with you and will bless you and multiply your descendants for my servant Abraham's sake."

GENESIS 26:24 RSV

Unless the Lord builds a house, the work of the builders is wasted. Unless the Lord protects a city, guarding it with sentries will do no good. It is useless for you to work so hard from early morning until late at night, anxiously working for food to eat; for God gives rest to his loved ones.

PSALM 127:1–2 NLT

The young lions lack and suffer hunger; but those who seek the Lord shall not lack any good thing.

PSALM 34:10

We pay for the water we drink, and our wood comes at a price. They pursue at our heels; we labor and have no rest. . . . Turn us back to You, O Lord, and we will be restored; renew our days as of old.

LAMENTATIONS 5:4–5, 21

They will live around my holy mountain, and I will bless
them by sending more than enough rain to make their trees
produce fruit and their crops to grow. I will set them free
from slavery and let them live safely in their own land.
Then they will know that I am the LORD. Foreign nations
will never again rob them, and wild animals will no longer
kill and eat them. They will have nothing to fear. I will
make their fields produce large amounts of crops, so they
will never again go hungry or be laughed at by foreigners.

EZEKIEL 34:26–29 CEV

I have been young, and now am old; yet I have not seen the
righteous forsaken, nor his descendants begging bread.

PSALM 37:25

"Yes, fields will once again be bought and sold—deeds signed
and sealed and witnessed—in the land of Benjamin and here
in Jerusalem, in the towns of Judah and in the hill country,
in the foothills of Judah and in the Negev, too. For someday
I will restore prosperity to them. I, the LORD, have spoken!"

JEREMIAH 32:44 NLT

Get all the advice and instruction you can, so
you will be wise the rest of your life.

PROVERBS 19:20 NLT

Now Jesus sat opposite the treasury and saw how the people put money into the treasury. And many who were rich put in much. Then one poor widow came and threw in two mites, which make a quadrans. So He called His disciples to Himself and said to them, "Assuredly, I say to you that this poor widow has put in more than all those who have given to the treasury; for they all put in out of their abundance, but she out of her poverty put in all that she had, her whole livelihood."

MARK 12:41–44

Your righteousness, O God, reaches to the highest heavens. You have done such wonderful things. Who can compare with you, O God? You have allowed me to suffer much hardship, but you will restore me to life again and lift me up from the depths of the earth. You will restore me to even greater honor and comfort me once again.

PSALM 71:19–21 NLT

Not that I speak in regard to need, for I have learned in whatever state I am, to be content.

PHILIPPIANS 4:11

I am the LORD your God. I rescued you from Egypt. Just ask, and I will give you whatever you need.

PSALM 81:10 CEV

*Consider the lilies, how they grow; they neither
toil nor spin; yet I tell you, even Solomon in all
his glory was not arrayed like one of these.*

LUKE 12:27 RSV

*Better a little with the fear of the LORD
than great wealth with turmoil.*

PROVERBS 15:16 NIV

*Turn and come to my rescue. Show your
wonderful love and save me, LORD.*

PSALM 6:4 CEV

*"But if God so clothes the grass of the field, which is alive today and
tomorrow is thrown into the furnace, will He not much more clothe
you? You of little faith! Do not worry then, saying, 'What will we
eat?' or 'What will we drink?' or 'What will we wear for clothing?'
For the Gentiles eagerly seek all these things; for your heavenly Father
knows that you need all these things. But seek first His kingdom
and His righteousness, and all these things will be added to you."*

MATTHEW 6:30–33 NASB

*Ascribe to the LORD the glory due his name; worship the LORD
in the splendor of his holiness. . . . The LORD sits enthroned over
the flood; the LORD is enthroned as King forever. The LORD gives
strength to his people; the LORD blesses his people with peace.*

PSALM 29:2, 10–11 NIV

Don't bargain with God. Be direct. Ask for what you need.
This isn't a cat-and-mouse, hide-and-seek game we're in. If
your child asks for bread, do you trick him with sawdust?
If he asks for fish, do you scare him with a live snake on his
plate? As bad as you are, you wouldn't think of such a thing.
You're at least decent to your own children. So don't you think
the God who conceived you in love will be even better?

MATTHEW 7:11 MSG

You will keep him in perfect peace, whose mind is
stayed on You, because he trusts in You.

ISAIAH 26:3

Only God gives inward peace, and I depend on him.

PSALM 62:5 CEV

That evening quail came and covered the camp, and in the morning
there was a layer of dew around the camp. When the dew was
gone, thin flakes like frost on the ground appeared on the desert
floor. When the Israelites saw it, they said to each other, "What
is it?" For they did not know what it was. . . . The people of Israel
called the bread manna. It was white like coriander seed and
tasted like wafers made with honey. Moses said, "This is what
the LORD has commanded: 'Take an omer of manna and keep
it for the generations to come, so they can see the bread I gave
you to eat in the wilderness when I brought you out of Egypt.'"

EXODUS 16:13–15, 31–32 NIV

*And my God shall supply all your need according
to His riches in glory by Christ Jesus.*

PHILIPPIANS 4:19

*Money that comes easily disappears quickly, but
money that is gathered little by little will grow.*

PROVERBS 13:11 NCV

*"And it will be that you [Elijah] shall drink from the
brook, and I have commanded the ravens to feed you
there." So he went and did according to the word of the
LORD, for he went and stayed by the Brook Cherith,
which flows into the Jordan. The ravens brought him
bread and meat in the morning, and bread and meat
in the evening; and he drank from the brook.*

1 KINGS 17:4–6

All hard work brings a profit, but mere talk leads only to poverty.

PROVERBS 14:23 NIV

*Don't love money; be satisfied with what you have. For God
has said, "I will never fail you. I will never abandon you."*

HEBREWS 13:5 NLT

*That evening the disciples came to him and said, "It
is already past time for supper, and there is nothing
to eat here in the desert; send the crowds away so
they can go to the villages and buy some food."
But Jesus replied, "That isn't necessary—you feed them!"
"What!" they exclaimed. "We have exactly five
small loaves of bread and two fish!"
"Bring them here," he said.
Then he told the people to sit down on the grass; and he took
the five loaves and two fish, looked up into the sky, and asked
God's blessing on the meal, then broke the loaves apart and
gave them to the disciples to place before the people. And
everyone ate until full! And when the scraps were picked
up afterwards, there were twelve basketfuls left over!*

MATTHEW 14:15–20 TLB

*And she said, "As the Lord your God lives, I have nothing baked,
only a handful of flour in a jar and a little oil in a jug. And now
I am gathering a couple of sticks that I may go in and prepare it
for myself and my son, that we may eat it and die." And Elijah
said to her, "Do not fear; go and do as you have said. But first
make me a little cake of it and bring it to me, and afterward make
something for yourself and your son. . . . And she went and did as
Elijah said. And she and he and her household ate for many days.
The jar of flour was not spent, neither did the jug of oil become
empty, according to the word of the Lord that he spoke by Elijah.*

1 KINGS 17:12–13, 15–16 ESV

*Cry out for insight, and ask for understanding. Search for them as you would for silver; seek them like hidden treasures. Then you will understand what it means to fear the L*ORD*, and you will gain knowledge of God. For the L*ORD *grants wisdom! From his mouth come knowledge and understanding.*

PROVERBS 2:3–6 NLT

The wicked man does deceptive work, but he who sows righteousness will have a sure reward.

PROVERBS 11:18

I know how to be abased, and I know how to abound. Everywhere and in all things I have learned both to be full and to be hungry, both to abound and to suffer need. I can do all things through Christ who strengthens me.

PHILIPPIANS 4:12–13

For our present troubles are small and won't last very long. Yet they produce for us a glory that vastly outweighs them and will last forever!

2 CORINTHIANS 4:17 NLT

FEAR NOT

God Is in Control

In this dangerous day, on this Fabergé-fragile globe, with financial collapse on the news and terrorists on the loose, we have every reason to retreat into bunkers of dread and woe. But Christ says to us, "See to it that you are not alarmed" (Matthew 24:6 NIV).

"Keep your head and don't panic" (MSG).

"See that you are not troubled" (NKJV).

"Be faithful unto death, and I will give you the crown of life" (Revelation 2:10 RSV).

All events, even the most violent, are under a divine plan. Every trial and trouble has a place in God's scheme.

Fearless

Do not be afraid of sudden terror,
nor of trouble from the wicked when it comes;
for the LORD will be your confidence,
and will keep your foot from being caught.

PROVERBS 3:25–26

I considered all this in my heart,
so that I could declare it all:
that the righteous and the wise and their works
are in the hand of God.

ECCLESIASTES 9:1

Your Redeemer is the Holy One of Israel;
He is called the God of the whole earth.

ISAIAH 54:5

Being confident of this very thing,
that He who has begun a good work in you
will complete it until the day of Jesus Christ.

PHILIPPIANS 1:6

~

Know that the LORD, He is God;
it is He who has made us, and not we ourselves;
we are His people and the sheep of His pasture.

PSALM 100:3

~

He is a shield to those who put their trust in Him.

PROVERBS 30:5

We need to hear that God is still in control. We need to hear that it's not over until he says so. We need to hear that life's mishaps and tragedies are not a reason to bail out. They are simply a reason to sit tight.

Corrie ten Boom used to say, "When the train goes through a tunnel and the world gets dark, do you jump out? Of course not. You sit still and trust the engineer to get you through."

Next time you're disappointed, don't panic. Don't jump out. Don't give up. Just be patient and let God remind you he's still in control.

He Still Moves Stones

*"These things I have spoken to you, that in Me
you may have peace. In the world
you will have tribulation; but be of good cheer,
I have overcome the world."*

JOHN 16:33

*Nothing can ever separate us from God's love. Neither
death nor life, neither angels nor demons, neither our fears
for today nor our worries about tomorrow—not even the
powers of hell can separate us from God's love.*

ROMANS 8:38 NLT

*They cried out to the LORD in their trouble,
and He saved them out of their distresses.*

PSALM 107:19

Don't Christ-followers enjoy a calendar full of Caribbean cruises? No.

Disciples can expect rough seas and stout winds. "In the world you will [not might, may, or could] have tribulation" (John 16:33, brackets mine).

Christ-followers contract malaria, bury children, battle addictions, and, as a result, face fears. It's not the absence of storms that sets us apart. It's whom we discover in the storm: an unstirred Christ.

Fearless

*You have been
my defense and
refuge in the day
of my trouble.*

PSALM 59:16

You may be down to your last paycheck, solution, or thimble of faith. Each sunrise seems to bring fresh reasons for fear.

They're talking layoffs at work, slowdowns in the economy, flare-ups in the Middle East, turnovers at headquarters, downturns in the housing market, upswings in global warming, breakouts of al Qaeda cells. Some demented dictator is collecting nuclear warheads the way others collect fine wines. A strain of Asian flu is boarding flights out of China. The plague of our day, terrorism, begins with the word *terror*.

But Jesus doesn't want you to live in a state of fear. Nor do you.

Fearless

He will cover you with his feathers,
and under his wings you can hide.
His truth will be your shield and protection.
You will not fear any danger by night
or an arrow during the day.

PSALM 91:4–5 NCV

~~

I called on the LORD in distress;
the LORD answered me and set me in a broad place.
The LORD is on my side;
I will not fear.
What can man do to me?

PSALM 118:5–6

Two types of voices command your attention today. Negative ones fill your mind with doubt, bitterness, and fear.

Positive ones purvey hope and strength.

Which ones will you choose to heed? You have a choice, you know. "We take every thought captive so that it is obedient to Christ" (2 Corinthians 10:5 GOD'S WORD).

Every Day Deserves a Chance

Be careful what you think,
because your thoughts run your life.

PROVERBS 4:23 NCV

～

Whatever things are true, whatever things
are noble, whatever things are just,
whatever things are pure, whatever things are lovely,
whatever things are of good report, if there is any virtue and if
there is anything praiseworthy—
meditate on these things.

PHILIPPIANS 4:6–8

～

Commit your works to the LORD,
and your thoughts will be established.

PROVERBS 16:3

*Fear not . . . be glad and rejoice, for the L*ORD
has done marvelous things!

JOEL 2:21

When you pass through the waters, I will be with you;
and through the rivers, they shall not overflow you.
When you walk through the fire, you shall not be burned,
nor shall the flame scorch you.
*For I am the L*ORD *your God,*
the Holy One of Israel, your Savior.

ISAIAH 43:2–3

The angel said to him, "Do not be afraid, Zacharias,
for your prayer is heard; and your wife Elizabeth will bear you a
son, and you shall call his name John."

LUKE 1:13

Make friends with whatever's next.

Embrace it. Accept it. Don't resist it.

Change is not only a part of life; change is a necessary part of God's strategy. To use us to change the world, he alters our assignments. Gideon: from farmer to general; Mary: from peasant girl to the mother of Christ; Paul: from local rabbi to world evangelist. God transitioned Joseph from a baby brother to an Egyptian prince. He changed David from a shepherd to a king.

Fearless

Be strong and brave, and do the work.
Don't be afraid or discouraged, because
the LORD God, my God, is with you.

1 CHRONICLES 28:20 NCV

~

Rest in the LORD, and wait patiently for Him.

PSALM 37:7

~

Many, O LORD my God, are Your wonderful works
which You have done;
and Your thoughts toward us
cannot be recounted to You in order;
if I would declare and speak of them,
they are more than can be numbered.

PSALM 40:5

One way to stop your worries is to *compile a worry list*. Over a period of days, record your anxious thoughts. Maintain a list of all the things that trouble you. Then review them. How many of them turned into a reality?

You worried that the house would burn down. Did it? That your job would be outsourced. Was it?

Next, *evaluate your worry categories.* Your list will highlight themes of worry. You'll detect recurring areas of preoccupation that may become obsessions: what people think of you, finances, global calamities, your appearance or performance. Pray specifically about them.

Fearless

*Thus says the L*ORD *who made you*
and formed you from the womb,
who will help you: "Fear not."

ISAIAH 44:2

∼

These little troubles are getting us ready
for an eternal glory that will make all our troubles
seem like nothing.

2 CORINTHIANS 4:17 CEV

∼

Oh, the depth of the riches both of the wisdom
and knowledge of God! How unsearchable
are His judgments and His ways past finding out!

ROMANS 11:33

What about the tragic changes God permits? When children are sexually abused or the sick lose their dignity . . . do such moments serve a purpose? They do if we see them from an eternal perspective. What makes no sense in this life will make perfect sense in the next. I have proof: you in the womb.

Some prenatal features went unused before birth. You grew a nose but didn't breathe. Eyes developed, but could you see? Your tongue, toenails, and crop of hair served no function in your mother's belly. But aren't you glad you have them now?

Certain chapters in this life seem so unnecessary. Holocausts. Martyrdom. Monsoons. If we assume this world exists just for pregrave happiness, these atrocities disqualify it from doing so. But what if this earth is the womb? Might these challenges, severe as they may be, serve to prepare us, equip us for the world to come?

Fearless

This is God, our God forever and ever;
He will be our guide even to death.

PSALM 48:14

Your hands have made me and fashioned me;
give me understanding, that I may learn
Your commandments.
Those who fear You will be glad when they see me,
because I have hoped in Your word.

PSALM 119:73–74

God will redeem my soul from the power of the grave,
for He shall receive me.

PSALM 49:15

Is your fear of dying robbing your joy of living? Jesus came to deliver those "who have lived their lives as slaves to the fear of dying" (Hebrews 2:15 NLT).

Death sits well within his jurisdiction. Morticians answer to him. "Christ died and rose again for this very purpose—to be Lord both of the living and of the dead" (Romans 14:9 NLT). Your death may surprise you and sadden others, but heaven knows no untimely death: "You saw me before I was born. Every day of my life was recorded in your book. Every moment was laid out before a single day had passed" (Psalm 139:16 NLT).

Come Thirsty

I am like a green olive tree in the house of God;
I trust in the mercy of God forever and ever.
I will praise You forever,
because You have done it;
and in the presence of Your saints
I will wait on Your name, for it is good.

PSALM 52:8–9

~

He offered up prayers and petitions with loud cries
and tears to the one who could save him from death.

HEBREWS 5:7 NIV

~

And this is the boldness we have in God's presence:
that if we ask God for anything that agrees with what he wants,
he hears us. If we know he hears us every time we ask him, we
know we have what we ask from him.

1 JOHN 5:14–15 NCV

Jesus made his fears public. He "offered up prayers and petitions with loud cries and tears to the one who could save him from death" (Hebrews 5:7 NIV). He prayed loudly enough to be heard and recorded, and he begged his community of friends to pray with him.

His prayer in the garden becomes, for Christians, a picture of the church in action—a place where fears can be verbalized, pronounced, stripped down, and denounced; an escape from the "wordless darkness" of suppressed frights. A healthy church is where our fears go to die. We pierce them through with Scripture, psalms of celebration and lament. We melt them in the sunlight of confession. We extinguish them with the waterfall of worship, choosing to gaze at God, not our dreads.

The big deal (and good news) is this: you needn't live alone with your fear.

Fearless

The ways of man are before the eyes of the LORD,
and He ponders all his paths.

PROVERBS 5:21

He who dwells in the shelter of the Most High
will rest in the shadow of the Almighty.
I will say of the LORD, "He is my refuge and my fortress,
my God, in whom I trust."

PSALM 91:1–2 NIV

God is able to make all grace abound toward you,
that you, always having all sufficiency in all things,
may have an abundance for every good work.

2 CORINTHIANS 9:8

If only we could order life the way we order gourmet coffee. Wouldn't you love to mix and match the ingredients of your future?

"Give me a tall, extra-hot cup of adventure, cut the dangers, with two shots of good health."

"A decaf brew of longevity, please, with a sprinkle of fertility. Go heavy on the agility and cut the disability."

"I'll go with a *grande* happy-latte, with a dollop of love sprinkled with Caribbean retirement."

Take me to *that* coffee shop. Too bad it doesn't exist. Truth is, life often hands us a concoction entirely different from the one we requested.

Life comes caffeinated with surprises. Modifications. Transitions. Alterations.

Fearless

When they saw Him walking
on the sea, they supposed it was a ghost,
and cried out. . . . But immediately
He talked with them and said to them,
"Be of good cheer! It is I; do not be afraid."

MARK 6:49–50

~

The LORD's hand is not shortened,
that it cannot save;
nor His ear heavy,
that it cannot hear.

ISAIAH 59:1

*Be strong and
of good courage;
do not fear nor
be dismayed.*

1 CHRONICLES 22:13

Feed your fears, and your faith will starve.

Feed your faith, and your fears will.

Jesus could have calmed your storm long ago. But he hasn't. Does he want to teach you a lesson? Could that lesson read something like this: "Storms are not an option, but fear is"?

God has recorded his accomplishments in Scripture. His résumé includes Red Sea openings. Lions' mouths closings. Goliath topplings. Lazarus raisings. Storm stillings and strollings.

His lesson is clear. He's the commander of every storm.

Fearless

I have loved you. . . . Fear not,
for I am with you.

ISAIAH 43:4–5

Yea, though I walk through the valley
of the shadow of death,
I will fear no evil;
for You are with me;
Your rod and Your staff, they comfort me.

PSALM 23:4

He humbled himself and became obedient
to death—even death on a cross!

PHILIPPIANS 2:8 NIV

Crucifixion was ugly and vile, harsh and degrading. And it was the manner by which Jesus chose to die. "He humbled himself and became obedient to death—even death on a cross!" (Philippians 2:8 NIV).

A calmer death would have sufficed. A single drop of blood could have redeemed humankind. Shed his blood, silence his breath, still his pulse, but be quick about it. Did the atonement for sin demand six hours of violence?

No, but his triumph over sadism did. Jesus once and for all displayed his authority over savagery. Evil may have her moments, but they will be brief. The master of death could not destroy the Lord of life. Heaven's best took hell's worst and turned it into hope.

Fearless

The Lord himself will come down from heaven
with a loud command, with the voice of the archangel,
and with the trumpet call of God.

1 THESSALONIANS 4:16 NCV

~

God will wipe away every tear from their eyes;
there shall be no more death, nor sorrow,
nor crying. There shall be no more pain,
for the former things have passed away.

REVELATION 21:4

~

[Christ] heals the brokenhearted
and binds up their wounds.

PSALM 147:3

An intriguing verse is found in 1 Thessalonians 4:16, "The Lord himself will come down from heaven with a loud command" (NCV).

Have you ever wondered what that command will be? It will be the inaugural word of heaven.

I could very well be wrong, but I think the command that puts an end to the pains of the earth and initiates the joys of heaven will be two words: "No more."

No more loneliness.

No more tears. No more fears.

No more death. No more sadness. No more crying. No more pain.

And the Angels Were Silent

Fearing people is a dangerous trap,
but trusting the LORD means safety.

PROVERBS 29:25 NLT

~

You are my hiding place;
you will protect me from trouble
and surround me with songs of deliverance.

PSALM 32:7 NIV

~

Do not fear any of those things
which you are about to suffer. . . . Be faithful until death,
and I will give you the crown of life.

REVELATION 2:10

Contrary to what we'd hope, good people aren't exempt from violence. Murderers don't give the godly a pass. Rapists don't vet victims according to spiritual résumés. The bloodthirsty and wicked don't skip over the heavenbound. We aren't insulated. But neither are we intimidated. Jesus has a word or two about this brutal world: "Do not fear those who kill the body but cannot kill the soul" (Matthew 10:28).

The disciples needed this affirmation. Jesus had just told them to expect scourging, trials, death, hatred, and persecution (vv. 17–23). Not the kind of locker-room pep talk that rallies the team. To their credit none defected.

Courage emerges, not from increased police security, but from enhanced spiritual maturity.

Fearless

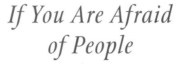

If You Are Afraid
of People

*"Listen to Me, you who know righteousness, You
people in whose heart is My law: Do not fear the
reproach of men, nor be afraid of their insults."*

ISAIAH 51:7

*Isaiah said these things because he saw the glory of
Christ, and spoke about him. Nevertheless, many even
of the authorities did believe in him. But they would not
admit it for fear of the Pharisees, in case they should be
excommunicated. They were more concerned to have the
approval of men than to have the approval of God.*

JOHN 12:41–43 PHILLIPS

*If you are reproached for the name of Christ, blessed are
you, for the Spirit of glory and of God rests upon you.*

1 PETER 4:14

*Arise, O LORD! Rescue me, my God! Slap all my enemies
in the face! Shatter the teeth of the wicked! Victory comes
from you, O LORD. May you bless your people.*

PSALM 3:7–8 NLT

David said to the Philistine, "You come against me with
sword and spear and javelin, but I come against you in the
name of the LORD Almighty, the God of the armies of Israel,
whom you have defied. This day the LORD will deliver
you into my hands, and I'll strike you down. . . .
All those gathered here will know that it is not by
sword or spear that the LORD saves; for the battle is the
LORD's, and he will give all of you into our hands."

1 SAMUEL 17:45–47 NIV

And Moses said to the people, "Fear not, stand
firm, and see the salvation of the LORD, which he
will work for you today; for the Egyptians whom
you see today, you shall never see again."

EXODUS 14:13 RSV

Then Asa called to the LORD his God and said,
"LORD, there is no one like you to help the powerless
against the mighty. Help us, LORD our God, for
we rely on you, and in your name we have come
against this vast army. LORD, you are our God;
do not let mere mortals prevail against you."

2 CHRONICLES 14:11 NIV

In God, whose word I praise—in God I trust and
am not afraid. What can mere mortals do to me?

PSALM 56:4 NIV

You, LORD, are the light that keeps me safe. I am not afraid of anyone. You protect me, and I have no fears.

PSALM 27:1 CEV

"'Fear not, for I am with you; be not dismayed, for I am your God. I will strengthen you, yes, I will help you, I will uphold you with My righteous right hand.' Behold, all those who were incensed against you shall be ashamed and disgraced; they shall be as nothing, and those who strive with you shall perish. You shall seek them and not find them—those who contended with you. Those who war against you shall be as nothing, as a nonexistent thing. For I, the LORD your God, will hold your right hand, saying to you, 'Fear not, I will help you.'"

ISAIAH 41:10–13

The LORD said: Israel, don't be afraid. Someday I will bring you home from foreign lands. You and your descendants will live in peace and safety, with nothing to fear.

JEREMIAH 46:27 CEV

God will command his angels to protect you wherever you go. They will carry you in their arms, and you won't hurt your feet on the stones. You will overpower the strongest lions and the most deadly snakes.

PSALM 91:11–13 CEV

The LORD is on my side; I will not fear. What can man do to me?

PSALM 118:6

This is how the LORD responds: "If you return to me, I will restore you so you can continue to serve me. If you speak good words rather than worthless ones, you will be my spokesman. You must influence them; do not let them influence you!"

JEREMIAH 15:19 NLT

Though I walk in the midst of trouble, You will revive me; you will stretch out Your hand against the wrath of my enemies, and Your right hand will save me.

PSALM 138:7

Turn from evil and do good; seek peace and pursue it. The eyes of the LORD are on the righteous, and his ears are attentive to their cry.

PSALM 34:14–15 NIV

Do not rebel against the LORD, and don't be afraid of the people of the land. They are only helpless prey to us! They have no protection, but the LORD is with us! Don't be afraid of them!

NUMBERS 14:9 NLT

He rescued me from my powerful enemy, from my foes, who were too strong for me. They confronted me in the day of my disaster, but the LORD was my support. He brought me out into a spacious place; he rescued me because he delighted in me.

2 SAMUEL 22:18–20 NIV

*Wait on the L*ORD*, and keep His way, and He shall exalt you to inherit the land; when the wicked are cut off, you shall see it.*

PSALM 37:34

*Thus says the L*ORD *to you: "Do not be afraid nor dismayed because of this great multitude, for the battle is not yours, but God's. . . . You will not need to fight in this battle. Position yourselves, stand still and see the salvation of the L*ORD*, who is with you, O Judah and Jerusalem!" Do not fear or be dismayed; tomorrow go out against them, for the L*ORD *is with you.*

2 CHRONICLES 20:15, 17

Blessed are you when people insult you and persecute you, and falsely say all kinds of evil against you because of Me. Rejoice and be glad, for your reward in heaven is great; for in the same way they persecuted the prophets who were before you.

MATTHEW 5:11–12 NASB

Don't judge others, and you will not be judged. Don't accuse others of being guilty, and you will not be accused of being guilty. Forgive, and you will be forgiven.

LUKE 6:37 NCV

*From the tents of God's people come shouts of victory: "The L*ORD *is powerful! With his mighty arm the L*ORD *wins victories! The L*ORD *is powerful!" And so my life is safe, and I will live to tell what the L*ORD *has done.*

PSALM 118:15–17 CEV

*I have confidence in you, in the Lord, that you
will have no other mind; but he who troubles you
shall bear his judgment, whoever he is.*

GALATIANS 5:10

*When I pray, LORD God, my enemies will retreat, because I
know for certain that you are with me. I praise your promises!
I trust you and am not afraid. No one can harm me.*

PSALM 56:9–11 CEV

*And all this assembly shall know that the Lord
saves not with sword and spear; for the battle is the
Lord's, and He will give you into our hands.*

1 SAMUEL 17:47 AMP

*Be still, and know that I am God: I will be exalted
among the heathen, I will be exalted in the earth.*

PSALM 46:10 KJV

*"Blessed be the name of God forever and ever, for wisdom
and might are His. And He changes the times and the
seasons; He removes kings and raises up kings; He gives
wisdom to the wise and knowledge to those who have
understanding. He reveals deep and secret things; He knows
what is in the darkness, and light dwells with Him."*

DANIEL 2:20–22

*If people say, "I love God," but hate their brothers or sisters, they
are liars. Those who do not love their brothers and sisters, whom
they have seen, cannot love God, whom they have never seen.*

1 JOHN 4:20 NCV

*I have set the LORD continually before me; because
He is at my right hand, I will not be shaken.*

PSALM 16:8 NASB

*"It is mine to avenge; I will repay. In due time their foot will slip;
their day of disaster is near and their doom rushes upon them."*

DEUTERONOMY 32:35 NIV

*Many are the sorrows of the wicked, but he who trusts
in, relies on, and confidently leans on the Lord shall be
compassed about with mercy and with loving-kindness.*

PSALM 32:10 AMP

*But to you who are listening I say: Love your
enemies, do good to those who hate you.*

LUKE 6:27 NIV

*I know that you are pleased with me, for my enemy
does not triumph over me. Because of my integrity you
uphold me and set me in your presence forever.*

PSALM 41:11–12 NIV

FEAR NOT

God Cares About You

Fear corrodes our confidence in God's goodness. We begin to wonder if love lives in heaven.

And it turns us into control freaks. Fear, at its center, is a perceived loss of control. When life spins wildly, we grab for a component of life we can manage: our diet, the tidiness of a house, the armrest of a plane, or, in many cases, people. The more insecure we feel, the meaner we become. We growl and bare our fangs. Why? Because we are bad? In part. But also because we feel cornered.

Fear creates a form of spiritual amnesia. It dulls our miracle memory. It makes us forget what Jesus has done and how good God is.

Fearless

[Jesus] arose and rebuked the wind,
and said to the sea, "Peace, be still!"
And the wind ceased and there was a great calm.
But He said to them, "Why are you so fearful?
How is it that you have no faith?"

MARK 4:39–40

The LORD himself will go before you.
He will be with you; he will not leave you or forget you.
Don't be afraid and don't worry.

DEUTERONOMY 31:8 NCV

"Don't let your hearts be troubled. Trust in God,
and trust also in me. . . . I will come and get you,
so that you will always be with me where I am."

JOHN 14:1, 3 NLT

Delight yourselves in God,
yes, find your joy in him at all times.

PHILIPPIANS 4:4 PHILLIPS

Jesus . . . said to the ruler of the synagogue,
"Do not be afraid; only believe."

MARK 5:36

By faith Moses, when he was born,
was hidden three months by his parents,
because they saw he was a beautiful child;
and they were not afraid of the king's command.

HEBREWS 11:23

The presence of fear does not mean you have no faith. Fear visits everyone. Even Christ was afraid (Mark 14:33). But make your fear a visitor and not a resident. Hasn't fear taken enough? Enough smiles? Chuckles? Restful nights, exuberant days? Meet your fears with faith.

Don't be afraid; just believe.

Believe that God can; believe that he cares.

Every Day Deserves a Chance

"With God nothing will be impossible."

LUKE 1:37

～

Great is our Lord, and mighty in power;
His understanding is infinite.

PSALM 147:5

～

I love the LORD,
because he listens to my prayers for help.
He paid attention to me,
so I will call to him for help as long as I live.

PSALM 116:1–2 NCV

Simple prayer equipped Christ to stare down his deepest fear.

Do likewise. Those persistent, ugly villains of the heart—talk to God about them. Specifically. Putting worries into words disrobes them. They look silly standing there naked.

It's our duty to pull back the curtains, to expose our fears, each and every one. Like vampires, they can't stand the sunlight. Financial fears, relationship fears, professional fears, safety fears—call them out in prayer. Drag them out by the hand of your mind, and make them stand before God and take their comeuppance!

Fearless

*Every good
and every perfect
gift . . . comes down
from the Father
of lights.*

JAMES 1:17

If your father were Bill Gates
and your computer broke, where
would you turn?

If Stradivari were your dad and
your violin string snapped, to
whom would you go?

If your father is God and you have
a problem on your hands, what
do you do?

God's not bewildered. Go to him.
He is able to do what you can't.

Every Day Deserves a Chance

*To Him who is able to do
exceedingly abundantly above all that we ask
or think, according to the power that works in us,
to Him be glory in the church by Christ Jesus
to all generations, forever and ever.*

EPHESIANS 3:20–21

～

*Now Jesus and the ones he makes holy
have the same Father. That is why Jesus is not ashamed
to call them his brothers and sisters.*

HEBREWS 2:11 NLT

"Fear not, for I am with you;
be not dismayed, for I am your God.
I will strengthen you,
yes, I will help you,
I will uphold you with My righteous right hand."

ISAIAH 41:10

∼∽

By awesome deeds in righteousness You will answer us,
O God of our salvation.

PSALM 65:5

∼∽

"Call to Me, and I will answer you,
and show you great and mighty things."

JEREMIAH 33:3

What's your worst fear? A fear of public failure, unemployment, or heights? The fear that you'll never find the right spouse or enjoy good health? The fear of being trapped, abandoned, or forgotten? These are real fears, born out of legitimate concerns. Yet left unchecked, they metastasize into obsessions.

The step between prudence and paranoia is short and steep. Prudence wears a seat belt. Paranoia avoids cars. Prudence washes with soap. Paranoia avoids human contact. Prudence saves for old age. Paranoia hoards even trash. Prudence prepares and plans. Paranoia panics. Prudence calculates the risk and takes the plunge. Paranoia never enters the water.

How many people spend life on the edge of the pool? Consulting caution. Ignoring faith. Never taking the plunge. For fear of the worst, they never enjoy life at its best.

Fearless

Do not fret because of evildoers,
nor be envious of the wicked;
for there will be no prospect for the evil man;
the lamp of the wicked will be put out.

PROVERBS 24:19–20

Weeping may endure for a night,
but joy comes in the morning.

PSALM 30:5

We are hard pressed on every side,
yet not crushed; we are perplexed,
but not in despair. . . . For our light affliction,
which is but for a moment, is working for us
a far more exceeding and eternal weight of glory. . . .
For the things which are seen are temporary,
but the things which are not seen are eternal.

2 CORINTHIANS 4:8, 17–18

Are you tied up in knots? "Cast all your anxiety on him because he cares for you" (1 Peter 5:7 NIV). Strong verb there. *Cast.* Not place, lay, or occasionally offer. Peter enlisted the same verb gospel writers used to describe the way Jesus treated demons. He cast them out. An authoritative hand on the collar, another on the belt, and a "Don't come back." Do the same with your fears. Get serious with them. Immediately cast them upon God.

Worry is an option, not an assignment. God can lead you into a worry-free world. Be quick to pray. Focus less on the problems ahead and more on the victories behind. Do your part, and God will do his. He will guard your heart with his peace . . . a peace that passes understanding.

Come Thirsty

*Your heavenly Father already knows
all your needs. Seek the Kingdom of God
above all else, and live righteously,
and he will give you everything you need.*

MATTHEW 6:32–33 NLT

~

*Let all those who seek You rejoice and be glad in You;
let such as love Your salvation say continually,
"The LORD be magnified!"*

PSALM 40:16

Seek the LORD and His strength; seek His face evermore!

1 CHRONICLES 16:11

Seek first the kingdom of wealth, and you'll worry over every dollar.

Seek first the kingdom of health, and you'll sweat every blemish and bump.

Seek first the kingdom of popularity, and you'll relive every conflict.

But seek first his kingdom, and you will find it. On that, we can depend and never worry.

Fearless

Some trust in chariots, and some in horses;
but we will remember the name of the LORD our God.

PSALM 20:7

~

When I remember You on my bed,
I meditate on You in the night watches.
Because You have been my help,
therefore in the shadow of Your wings I will rejoice.

PSALM 63:6–7

~

Seek the LORD and His strength;
seek His face evermore!
Remember His marvelous works which He has done,
His wonders, and the judgments of His mouth.

PSALM 105:4–5

In what was perhaps the last letter Paul ever wrote, he begged Timothy not to forget. You can almost picture the old warrior smiling as he wrote the words. "Remember Jesus Christ, raised from the dead, descended from David" (2 Timothy 2:8 NIV).

When times get hard, remember Jesus. When people don't listen, remember Jesus. When tears come, remember Jesus. When disappointment is your bed partner, remember Jesus. When fear pitches his tent in your front yard. When death looms, when anger singes, when shame weighs heavily. Remember Jesus.

Remember holiness in tandem with humanity. Remember the sick who were healed with callused hands. Remember the dead called from the grave with a Galilean accent. Remember the eyes of God that wept human tears.

Six Hours One Friday

Are not two sparrows sold for a penny?
Yet not one of them will fall to the ground
apart from the will of your Father. And even the very hairs of
your head are all numbered. So don't be afraid;
you are worth more than many sparrows.

MATTHEW 10:29–31 NIV

I will praise You, for I am fearfully
and wonderfully made; marvelous are Your works,
and that my soul knows very well.

PSALM 139:14

We are God's masterpiece.
He has created us anew in Christ Jesus,
so we can do the good things he planned for us long ago.

EPHESIANS 2:10 NLT

Do we matter? We fear we don't. We fear coming and going and no one knowing.

That's why it bothers us when a friend forgets to call or the teacher forgets our name or a colleague takes credit for something we've done. They are affirming our deepest trepidation: no one cares, because we aren't worth caring about.

If you pass your days mumbling, "I'll never make a difference; I'm not worth anything," guess what? You will be sentencing yourself to a life of gloom without parole.

Even more, you are disagreeing with God. According to him, you were "skillfully wrought" (Psalm 139:15). You were "fearfully and wonderfully made" (v. 14). He can't stop thinking about you! If you could count his thoughts of you, "they would be more in number than the sand" (v. 18).

Fearless

Though I walk through the valley of the shadow of death,
I will fear no evil;
for You are with me;
Your rod and Your staff, they comfort me.

PSALM 23:4

~

He is not far from each one of us;
for in Him we live and move and have our being.

ACTS 17:27–28

~

He made His own people go forth like sheep,
and guided them in the wilderness like a flock;
and He led them on safely, so that they did not fear;
but the sea overwhelmed their enemies.

PSALM 78:52–53

"I will fear no evil." How could David the Shepherd-King make such a claim? Because he knew where to look. "You are with me; Your rod and Your staff, they comfort me" (Psalm 23:4).

Rather than turn to the other sheep, David turned to the Shepherd. Rather than stare at the problems, he stared at the rod and staff. Because he knew where to look, David was able to say, "I will fear no evil."

Don't measure the size of the mountain; talk to the One who can move it. Instead of carrying the world on your shoulders, talk to the One who holds the universe on his. Hope is a look away.

Traveling Light

There is no fear in love;
but perfect love casts out fear,
because fear involves torment.
But he who fears
has not been made perfect in love.

1 JOHN 4:18

~

The angel of the LORD encamps
all around those who fear Him,
and delivers them.
Oh, taste and see that the LORD is good;
blessed is the man who trusts in Him!

PSALM 34:7–8

*He who heeds
the word wisely
will find good, and
whoever trusts
in the LORD,
happy is he.*

PROVERBS 16:20

Courage does not panic; it prays.

Courage does not bemoan; it believes.

Courage does not languish; it listens.

It listens to the voice of God. It hears Christ's voice comforting through the hospital corridors, graveyards, and war zones.

Fearless

*Anyone who is having troubles
should pray. Anyone who is happy
should sing praises.*

JAMES 5:13 NCV

*The young lions lack and suffer hunger;
but those who seek the LORD
shall not lack any good thing.*

PSALM 34:10

*It is better to take refuge in the LORD
than to trust in a man.*

PSALM 118:8 NIV

If you've ever had your spouse call you at the office and say, "Just got a letter from the IRS. They are going to audit."

If your boss has ever begun a conversation with these words: "You're a good worker, but with all this talk about a recession, we have to cut back."

Then you know that life can go from calm to chaos in a matter of moments.

Take heart. Jesus knows how you feel. J. B. Phillips translates Hebrews 4:15: "For we have no superhuman High Priest to whom our weaknesses are unintelligible—he himself has shared fully in all our experience of temptation, except that he never sinned."

Jesus shared fully *in all our experience*. Every hurt. Each ache. All the stresses and all the strains. No exceptions. No substitutes. Why? So he could sympathize with our weaknesses.

In the Eye of the Storm

God . . . does great things
which we cannot comprehend.

JOB 37:5

~

Though an army besiege me,
my heart will not fear;
though war break out against me,
even then will I be confident.

PSALM 27:3 NIV

~

What then shall we say to these things?
If God is for us, who can be against us?

ROMANS 8:31

Real courage embraces the twin realities of current difficulty and ultimate triumph. Yes, life stinks. But it won't forever. As one of my friends likes to say, "Everything will work out in the end. If it's not working out, it's not the end."

We gain nothing by glossing over the brutality of human existence. This is a toxic world. But neither do we join the Chicken Little chorus of gloom and doom. "The sky is falling! The sky is falling!" Somewhere between Pollyanna and Chicken Little, between blind denial and blatant panic, stands the levelheaded, clear-thinking, still-believing follower of Christ. Wide eyed, yet unafraid. Unterrified by the terrifying. The calmest kid on the block, not for lack of bullies, but for faith in his older Brother.

Fearless

But the Lord is faithful, who will establish you and guard you from the evil one.

2 THESSALONIANS 3:3

Being a parent is better than a course on theology. Being a father is teaching me that when I am criticized, injured, or afraid, there is a Father who is ready to comfort me. There is a Father who will hold me until I'm better, who will help me until I can live with the hurt, and who won't go to sleep when I'm afraid of waking up and seeing the dark.

Ever.

The Applause of Heaven

You will keep him in perfect peace,
whose mind is stayed on You,
because he trusts in You.

ISAIAH 26:3

～

Blessed be the God and Father of our Lord Jesus Christ, who
according to His abundant mercy
has begotten us again to a living hope
through the resurrection of Jesus Christ from the dead.

1 PETER 1:3

*[Jesus] said to His disciples, "Therefore I say to you,
do not worry about your life, what you will eat; nor about the
body, what you will put on. Life is more than food,
and the body is more than clothing. Consider the ravens, for
they neither sow nor reap, which have neither
storehouse nor barn; and God feeds them. Of how much more
value are you than the birds?"*

LUKE 12:22–24

*I have never seen the godly abandoned
or their children begging for bread.*

PSALM 37:25 NLT

*I have learned to be satisfied with the things I have
and with everything that happens. I know how to live
when I am poor, and I know how to live when I have plenty. I
have learned the secret of being happy at any time
in everything that happens. . . . I can do all things
through Christ, because he gives me strength.*

PHILIPPIANS 4:11–13 NCV

Accumulation of wealth is a popular defense against fear. Since we fear losing our jobs, health care, or retirement benefits, we amass possessions, thinking the more we have, the safer we are.

We engineer stock and investment levies, take cover behind the hedge of hedge funds. We trust annuities and pensions to the point that balance statements determine our mood levels. But then come the Katrina-level recessions and downturns, and the confusion begins all over again.

If there were no God, stuff-trusting would be the only appropriate response to an uncertain future. But there is a God. And this God does not want his children to trust money. "Do not worry about your life. . . . Do not seek what you should eat or what you should drink, nor have an anxious mind" (Luke 12:22, 29).

Fearless

He who is in you
is greater than he who is in the world.

1 JOHN 4:4

~

Let me hear Your lovingkindness in the morning;
For I trust in You.

PSALM 143:8 NASB

~

In quietness and trust is your strength.

ISAIAH 30:15 NIV

Jairus fell at Jesus' feet, saying again and again, "My daughter is dying. Please come and put your hands on her so she will be healed and will live" (Mark 5:23 NIV).

There are no games. No haggling. No masquerades. The situation is starkly simple: Jairus is blind to the future and Jesus knows the future. So Jairus asks for his help.

And Jesus, who loves the honest heart, goes to give it. . . . [He] turns immediately to Jairus and pleads: "Don't be afraid; just believe" (v. 36 NIV).

Jesus compels Jairus to see the unseen. When Jesus says, "Just believe . . . ," he is imploring, "Don't limit your possibilities to the visible. Don't listen only for the audible. Don't be controlled by the logical. Believe there is more to life than meets the eye!"

"Trust me," Jesus is pleading. "Don't be afraid; just trust."

He Still Moves Stones

Jesus said to them,
"Do not be afraid. Go and tell My brethren
to go to Galilee, and there they will see Me."

MATTHEW 28:10

~

The disciples heard it . . . and were greatly afraid.
But Jesus came and touched them
and said, "Arise, and do not be afraid."

MATTHEW 17:6–7

Jesus spoke to them, saying, "Be of good cheer! It is I; do not be afraid."

MATTHEW 14:27

The Gospels list some 125 Christ-issued imperatives. Of these, 21 urge us to "not be afraid" or "not fear" or "have courage" or "take heart" or "be of good cheer." The second most common command, to love God and neighbor, appears on only eight occasions. If quantity is any indicator, Jesus takes our fears seriously. The one statement he made more than any other was this: don't be afraid.

Fearless

If You are Afraid
of Death

*But those who die in the L*ORD *will live; their bodies will rise again! Those who sleep in the earth will rise up and sing for joy!*

ISAIAH 26:19 NLT

Yea, though I walk through the valley of the shadow of death, I will fear no evil: for thou art with me; thy rod and thy staff they comfort me.

PSALM 23:4 KJV

God saved us from these great dangers of death, and he will continue to save us. We have put our hope in him, and he will save us again.

2 CORINTHIANS 1:10 NCV

For I know that this will turn out for my deliverance through your prayers and the provision of the Spirit of Jesus Christ, according to my earnest expectation and hope, that I will not be put to shame in anything, but that with all boldness, Christ will even now, as always, be exalted in my body, whether by life or by death.

PHILIPPIANS 1:19–21 NASB

So we know and believe the love God has for us. God is love, and he who abides in love abides in God, and God abides in him. In this is love perfected with us, that we may have confidence for the day of judgment, because as he is so are we in this world.

1 JOHN 4:16–17 RSV

Reverent and worshipful fear of the Lord is a fountain of life, that one may avoid the snares of death.

PROVERBS 14:27 AMP

Since, therefore, [these His] children share in flesh and blood [in the physical nature of human beings], He [Himself] in a similar manner partook of the same [nature], that by [going through] death He might bring to nought and make of no effect him who had the power of death—that is, the devil—

And also that He might deliver and completely set free all those who through the [haunting] fear of death were held in bondage throughout the whole course of their lives.

HEBREWS 2:14–15 AMP

And I am convinced that nothing can ever separate us from God's love. Neither death nor life, neither angels nor demons, neither our fears for today nor our worries about tomorrow— not even the powers of hell can separate us from God's love.

ROMANS 8:38 NLT

*In the days of his flesh, Jesus offered up prayers and
supplications, with loud cries and tears, to him who was able
to save him from death, and he was heard for his godly fear.*

HEBREWS 5:7 RSV

*The wicked is overthrown through his wrongdoing
and calamity, but the [consistently] righteous
has hope and confidence even in death.*

PROVERBS 14:32 AMP

*Praise God, the Father of our Lord Jesus Christ.
God is so good, and by raising Jesus from death, he
has given us new life and a hope that lives on.*

1 PETER 1:3 CEV

*"God loved the world so much that he gave his
one and only Son so that whoever believes in him
may not be lost, but have eternal life."*

JOHN 3:16 NCV

*"Verily, verily, I say unto you, He that heareth
my word, and believeth on him that sent me,
hath everlasting life, and shall not come into
condemnation; but is passed from death unto life."*

JOHN 5:24 KJV

This is what God told us: God has given us
eternal life, and this life is in his Son.

1 JOHN 5:11 NCV

Jesus answered him, "Truly I tell you, today
you will be with me in paradise."

LUKE 23:43 NIV

"Teaching them to observe all that I have commanded you.
And behold, I am with you always, to the end of the age."

MATTHEW 28:20 ESV

Do not grieve the Holy Spirit of God, by whom you
were sealed for the day of redemption. Let all bitterness
and wrath and anger and clamor and slander be
put away from you, along with all malice.

EPHESIANS 4:30–31 NASB

I give them eternal life, and they will never perish,
and no one will snatch them out of my hand.

JOHN 10:28 ESV

But you, beloved, building yourselves up on your
most holy faith, praying in the Holy Spirit, keep
yourselves in the love of God, waiting anxiously for
the mercy of our Lord Jesus Christ to eternal life.

JUDE VV. 20–21 NASB

Now the law came in to increase the trespass, but where sin increased, grace abounded all the more, so that, as sin reigned in death, grace also might reign through righteousness leading to eternal life through Jesus Christ our Lord.

ROMANS 5:20–21 ESV

For, "Everyone who calls on the name of the Lord will be saved."

ROMANS 10:13 NIV

Now God has us where he wants us, with all the time in this world and the next to shower grace and kindness upon us in Christ Jesus. Saving is all his idea, and all his work. All we do is trust him enough to let him do it. It's God's gift from start to finish! We don't play the major role. If we did, we'd probably go around bragging that we'd done the whole thing! No, we neither make nor save ourselves. God does both the making and saving. He creates each of us by Christ Jesus to join him in the work he does, the good work he has gotten ready for us to do, work we had better be doing.

EPHESIANS 2:7–10 MSG

Those who live in the shelter of the Most High will find rest in the shadow of the Almighty.

PSALM 91:1 NLT

For those who follow godly paths will rest in peace when they die.

ISAIAH 57:2 NLT

And which of you by being anxious can add a cubit to his span of life? If then you are not able to do as small a thing as that, why are you anxious about the rest?

LUKE 12:25–26 RSV

Christ obeyed God our Father and gave himself as a sacrifice for our sins to rescue us from this evil world.

GALATIANS 1:4 CEV

Our God is a God who saves; from the Sovereign LORD comes escape from death.

PSALM 68:20 NIV

In Him, you also, after listening to the message of truth, the gospel of your salvation—having also believed, you were sealed in Him with the Holy Spirit of promise, who is given as a pledge of our inheritance, with a view to the redemption of God's own possession, to the praise of His glory.

EPHESIANS 1:13–14 NASB

"Truly I tell you, some who are standing here will not taste death before they see the Son of Man coming in his kingdom."

MATTHEW 16:28 NIV

He saved us, not because of righteous things we had done, but because of his mercy. He saved us through the washing of rebirth and renewal by the Holy Spirit, whom he poured out on us generously through Jesus Christ our Savior, so that, having been justified by his grace, we might become heirs having the hope of eternal life. This is a trustworthy saying. And I want you to stress these things, so that those who have trusted in God may be careful to devote themselves to doing what is good. These things are excellent and profitable for everyone.

TITUS 3:5–8 NIV

And so faith, hope, love abide [faith—conviction and belief respecting man's relation to God and divine things; hope— joyful and confident expectation of eternal salvation; love— true affection for God and man, growing out of God's love for and in us], these three; but the greatest of these is love.

1 CORINTHIANS 13:13 AMP

In view of the fact that all these things are to be dissolved, what sort of people ought you to be? Surely men of good and holy character, who live expecting and earnestly longing for the coming of the day of God. True, this day will mean that the heavens will disappear in fire and the elements disintegrate in fearful heat, but our hopes are set not on these but on the new Heaven and the new earth which he has promised us, and in which nothing but good shall live.

2 PETER 3:11–13 PHILLIPS

Our LORD and God, you are my lamp. You turn darkness to light. . . . Your way is perfect, LORD, and your word is correct. You are a shield for those who run to you for help.

2 SAMUEL 22:29, 31 CEV

Now may the God of hope fill you with all joy and peace in believing, so that you will abound in hope by the power of the Holy Spirit.

ROMANS 15:13 NASB

For the wages of sin is death, but the gift of God is eternal life in Christ Jesus our Lord.

ROMANS 6:23 NIV

Those who fear the LORD are secure; he will be a refuge for their children. Fear of the LORD is a life-giving fountain; it offers escape from the snares of death.

PROVERBS 14:26–27 NLT

FEAR NOT

God Loves and Forgives

Fear, mismanaged, leads to sin. Sin leads to hiding. Since we've all sinned, we all hide, not in bushes, but in eighty-hour workweeks, temper tantrums, and religious busyness. We avoid contact with God.

We are convinced that God must hate our evil tendencies. We draw a practical conclusion: God is irreparably ticked off at us.

[But] Jesus made forgiveness his first fearless announcement. Yes, we have disappointed God. But, no, God has not abandoned us.

Jesus loves us too much to leave us in doubt about his grace. His "perfect love expels all fear" (1 John 4:18 NLT). If God loved with an imperfect love, we would have high cause to worry. Imperfect love keeps a list of sins and consults it often. God keeps no list of our wrongs. His love casts out our fear because he casts out our sin!

Fearless

[His] perfect love expels all fear.

1 JOHN 4:18 NLT

He who believes in Him is not condemned.

JOHN 3:18

Everyone who looks to the Son
and believes in him shall have eternal life,
and I will raise him up at the last day.

JOHN 6:40 NIV

I am the LORD,
I do not change.

MALACHI 3:6

The next time you are mired in a bad day, check your outlook with these three reminders:

Yesterday ... forgiven.

Tomorrow ... surrendered.

Today ... clarified.

Jesus' design for a good day makes such sense. His grace erases guilt. His oversight removes fear. His direction removes confusion.

Every Day Deserves a Chance

Trust in the LORD with all your heart
and lean not on your own understanding;
in all your ways acknowledge him,
and he will make your paths straight.

PROVERBS 3:5–6 NIV

~

When times are good, be happy;
but when times are bad, consider:
God has made the one as well as the other.
Therefore, a man cannot discover
anything about his future.

ECCLESIASTES 7:14 NIV

Listen to Me, you who know righteousness,
you people in whose heart is My law:
Do not fear the reproach of men,
nor be afraid of their insults.

ISAIAH 51:7

The LORD is my rock and my fortress and my deliverer;
my God, my strength, in whom I will trust;
my shield and the horn of my salvation, my stronghold.

PSALM 18:2

He is the living God,
and steadfast forever;
His kingdom is the one which shall not be destroyed,
and His dominion shall endure to the end.
He delivers and rescues,
and He works signs and wonders
in heaven and on earth.

DANIEL 6:26–27

All things, big and small, flow out of the purpose of God and serve his good will. When the world appears out of control, it isn't. When warmongers appear to be in charge, they aren't. When ecological catastrophes dominate the day, don't let them dominate you.

Let's trust our heavenly Father. He has diagnosed the pain of the world and written the book on its treatment. We can trust him.

Fearless

*Whoever keeps His word, truly the love of God
is perfected in him. By this we know that we are in Him.
He who says he abides in Him ought himself also
to walk just as He walked.*

1 JOHN 2:5–6

～

*As for God, His way is perfect;
The word of the LORD is proven;
He is a shield to all who trust in Him.
For who is God, except the LORD?
And who is a rock, except our God?*

PSALM 18:30–31

～

*By one offering He has perfected forever
those who are being sanctified.*

HEBREWS 10:14

God views Christians the way he views Christ: sinless and perfect.

Don't fear he will discover your past. He already has.

Don't fear disappointing him in the future. He can show you the chapter in which you will.

With perfect knowledge of the past and perfect vision of the future, he loves you perfectly in spite of both.

Come Thirsty

You shall not be terrified of them;
*for the L*ord *your God, the great and awesome God,*
is among you.

DEUTERONOMY 7:21

～

He is your praise, and He is your God,
who has done for you these great and awesome things which
your eyes have seen.

DEUTERONOMY 10:21

～

Come and see the works of God;
He is awesome in His doing toward the sons of men.

PSALM 66:5

When Christ is great, our fears are not.

As awe of Jesus expands, fears of life diminish. A big God translates into big courage. A small view of God generates no courage. A limp, puny, fireless Jesus has no power over cancer cells, corruption, identity theft, stock-market crashes, or global calamity. A packageable, portable Jesus might fit well in a purse or on a shelf, but he does nothing for your fears.

Don't we need to know the transfigured Christ? [The] one who...occupies the loftiest perch and wears the only true crown of the universe, God's beloved Son?

The longer we live in him, the greater he becomes in us. It's not that he changes but that we do; we see more of him.

Fearless

—⁂—

Trust ye in the LORD for ever:
for in the LORD JEHOVAH is everlasting strength.

ISAIAH 26:4 KJV

The angel said to her, "Do not be afraid, Mary,
for you have found favor with God. And behold,
you will conceive in your womb and bring forth
a Son, and shall call His name JESUS."

LUKE 1:30–31

Behold, God is my salvation; I will trust,
and not be afraid: for the LORD JEHOVAH is my strength and my
song; he also is become my salvation.

ISAIAH 12:2 KJV

Here are just a few of the names of God that describe his character. Study them, for in any given day, you may need each one of them. Let me show you what I mean.

When you're confused about the future, go to your *Jehovah-raah*, your caring shepherd.

When you're anxious about provision, talk to *Jehovah-jireh*, the Lord who provides.

Are your challenges too great? Seek the help of *Jehovah-shalom,* the Lord is peace.

Is your body sick? Are your emotions weak? *Jehovah-rophe*, the Lord who heals you, will see you now.

Meditating on the names of God reminds you of the character of God. Take these names and bury them in your heart.

The Great House of God

Do not fear . . .
The LORD your God in your midst,
the Mighty One, will save;
He will rejoice over you with gladness,
He will quiet you with His love,
He will rejoice over you with singing.

ZEPHANIAH 3:16–17

~

As we live in God, our love grows more perfect.
So we will not be afraid on the day of judgment,
but we can face him with confidence because we live
like Jesus here in this world. Such love has no fear,
because perfect love expels all fear. If we are afraid,
it is for fear of punishment, and this shows that
we have not fully experienced his perfect love.

1 JOHN 4:17–18 NLT

The LORD has appeared of old to me, saying: "Yes, I have loved you with an everlasting love; therefore with lovingkindness I have drawn you."

JEREMIAH 31:3

We fear rejection, so we follow the crowd. We fear not fitting in, so we take the drugs. For fear of standing out, we wear what everyone else wears. For fear of blending in, we wear what no one else wears. For fear of sleeping alone, we sleep with anyone. For fear of not being loved, we search for love in all the wrong places.

But God flushes those fears. Those saturated in God's love don't sell out to win the love of others. They don't even sell out to win the love of God.

We all need improvement, but we don't need to woo God's love. We change because we already have God's love. God's perfect love.

Come Thirsty

*If we confess our sins, He is faithful and just
to forgive us our sins and to cleanse us
from all unrighteousness.*

1 JOHN 1:9

～

*Don't be afraid. It's true that you did wrong,
but don't turn away from the Lord. Serve the Lord
with all your heart.*

1 SAMUEL 12:20 NCV

～

*By grace you have been saved through faith . . .
it is the gift of God.*

EPHESIANS 2:8

Nothing fosters courage like a clear grasp of grace. And nothing fosters fear like an ignorance of mercy. May I speak candidly? If you haven't accepted God's forgiveness, you are doomed to fear. Nothing can deliver you from the gnawing realization that you have disregarded your Maker and disobeyed his instruction. No pill, pep talk, psychiatrist, or possession can set the sinner's heart at ease. You may deaden the fear, but you can't remove it. Only God's grace can.

Have you accepted the forgiveness of Christ? If not, do so. Your prayer can be as simple as this: *Dear Father, I need forgiveness. I admit that I have turned away from you. Please forgive me. I place my soul in your hands and my trust in your grace. Through Jesus I pray, amen.*

Having received God's forgiveness, live forgiven! When Jesus sets you free, you are free indeed.

Fearless

You should not be like cowering,
fearful slaves. You should behave instead
like God's very own children, adopted
into his family—calling him "Father, dear Father."

ROMANS 8:15 PHILLIPS

We have such trust through Christ toward God.
Not that we are sufficient of ourselves to think of anything as
being from ourselves, but our sufficiency is from God.

2 CORINTHIANS 3:4–5

The Lord will deliver me from every evil work
and preserve me for His heavenly kingdom.
To Him be glory forever and ever. Amen!

2 TIMOTHY 4:18

Your heavenly Father has no intention of letting you fall. You are "shielded by God's power" (1 Peter 1:5 NIV). He is "able to keep you from falling and to present you before his glorious presence without fault and with great joy" (Jude v. 24 NIV).

Drink deeply from this truth. God is able to keep you from falling! Does he want you living in fear? No! Just the opposite. "The Spirit we received does not make us slaves again to fear; it makes us children of God.... And the Spirit himself joins with our spirits to say we are God's children" (Romans 8:15–16 NCV).

Deep within you, God's Spirit confirms with your spirit that you belong to him. Beneath the vitals of the heart, God's Spirit whispers, "You are mine. I bought you and sealed you, and no one can take you."

Come Thirsty

We must not become tired of doing good.
We will receive our harvest of eternal life
at the right time if we do not give up.

GALATIANS 6:9 NCV

~~

My brothers and sisters, when you have
many kinds of troubles, you should be full of joy,
because you know that these troubles test your faith,
and this will give you patience.

JAMES 1:2–3 NCV

~~

Those people who keep their faith until the
end will be saved.

MATTHEW 10:22 NCV

If you live in a world darkened by sin, you may be its victim.

Jesus is honest about the life we are called to lead. There is no guarantee that just because we belong to him we will go unscathed. No promise is found in Scripture that says when you follow the king you are exempt from battle. No, often just the opposite is the case.

How do we survive the battle? How do we endure the fray?

Jesus says: "Those people who keep their faith until the end will be saved" (Matthew 24:13 NCV).

He doesn't say if you succeed you will be saved. Or if you come out on top you will be saved. He says if you endure.

And the Angels Were Silent

Those who wait on the LORD
shall renew their strength; they shall mount up
with wings like eagles, they shall run and not be weary, they
shall walk and not faint.

ISAIAH 40:31

~

Despite all these things, overwhelming victory is ours
through Christ, who loved us.

ROMANS 8:37 NLT

We have been sanctified through the offering of the body of Jesus Christ once for all.

God wants you to fly.

He wants you to fly free of yesterday's guilt.

He wants you to fly free of today's fears.

He wants you to fly free of tomorrow's grave.

Sin, fear, and death. These are the mountains he has moved. This is what he longs to do: he longs to set you free so you can fly.

And the Angels Were Silent

As the heavens are high above the earth,
so great is His mercy toward those who fear Him;
as far as the east is from the west,
so far has He removed our transgressions from us.

PSALM 103:11–12

~~

God's readiness to give and forgive is now public.
Salvation's available for everyone! . . . Tell them all this.
Build up their courage.

TITUS 2:11, 15 MSG

~~

When our hearts make us feel guilty, we can
still have peace before God. God is greater than our hearts,
and he knows everything.

1 JOHN 3:20 NCV

Tether your heart to this promise, and tighten the knot. Remember the words of John's epistle: "If our heart condemns us, God is greater than our heart, and knows all things" (1 John 3:20). When you feel unforgiven, evict the feelings. Emotions don't get a vote. Go back to Scripture. God's Word holds rank over self-criticism and self-doubt.

As Paul told Titus, "God's readiness to give and forgive is now public. Salvation's available for everyone! . . . Tell them all this. Build up their *courage*" (Titus 2:11, 15 MSG, emphasis mine). Do you know God's grace? Then you can love boldly, live robustly. You can swing from trapeze to trapeze; his safety net will break your fall.

Fearless

*Jesus said to her, "I am the resurrection and the life.
He who believes in Me, though he may die, he shall live. And
whoever lives and believes in Me shall never die."*

JOHN 11:25–26

*Blessed be the God and Father of our Lord
Jesus Christ, who according to His abundant mercy
has begotten us again to a living hope through
the resurrection of Jesus Christ from the dead.*

1 PETER 1:3

*We know that our body—the tent we live in
here on earth—will be destroyed. But when that happens, God
will have a house for us. It will not be a house made by human
hands; instead, it will be a home in heaven
that will last forever.*

2 CORINTHIANS 5:1 NCV

Death. The bully on the block of life. He catches you in the alley. He taunts you in the playground. He badgers you on the way home: "You, too, will die someday."

He'll make your stomach tighten. He'll leave you wide eyed and flat footed. He'll fence you in with fear. He'll steal the joy of your youth and the peace of your final years. And if he achieves what he sets out to do, he'll make you so afraid of dying that you never learn to live.

But the Christian can face the bully nose to nose and claim the promise that echoed in [Christ's] empty tomb, "My death is not final."

Six Hours One Friday

"Call upon Me in the day of trouble; I will deliver you, and you shall glorify Me."

PSALM 50:15

You may be facing death, but you aren't facing death alone; the Lord is with you.

You may be facing unemployment, but you aren't facing unemployment alone; the Lord is with you.

You may be facing marital struggles, but you aren't facing them alone; the Lord is with you.

You may be facing debt, but you aren't facing debt alone; the Lord is with you.

Traveling Light

Because God's children are human beings—made of flesh and blood—the Son also became flesh and blood. For only as a human being could he die, and only by dying could he break the power of the devil, who had the power of death. Only in this way could he set free all who have lived their lives as slaves to the fear of dying.

HEBREWS 2:14–15 NLT

∽

He Himself has said, "I will never leave you nor forsake you." So we may boldly say: "The LORD is my helper; I will not fear. What can man do to me?"

HEBREWS 13:5–6

He who began a good work in you
will carry it on to completion until the day of Christ Jesus.

PHILIPPIANS 1:6 NIV

~

May the God of peace . . . make you complete
in every good work to do His will.

HEBREWS 13:20–21

~

He who hears My word
and believes in Him who sent Me
has everlasting life.

JOHN 5:24

Religious rule keeping can sap your strength. It's
endless. There is always another class to attend, Sabbath
to obey, Ramadan to observe. No prison is as endless
as the prison of perfection. Her inmates find work but
never find peace. How could they? They never know
when they are finished.

Christ, however, gifts you with a finished work. He
fulfilled the law for you. Bid farewell to the burden of
religion. Gone is the fear that, having done everything,
you might not have done enough. You climb the stairs,
not by your strength, but his. God pledges to help those
who stop trying to help themselves.

Next Door Savior

I came that they may have life,
and have it abundantly.

JOHN 10:10 NASB

The LORD is near to all who call upon Him.

PSALM 145:18

"He who follows Me shall not walk in darkness,
but have the light of life."

JOHN 8:12

I wish we would take Jesus at his word. I wish,
like heaven, that we would learn that when he says
something, it happens.

When he says we're forgiven, let's unload the guilt.

When he says we're valuable, let's believe him.

When he says we're eternal, let's bury our fear.

When he says we're provided for, let's stop worrying.

He Still Moves Stones

He has made everything beautiful in its time.
He has also set eternity in the hearts of men;
yet they cannot fathom what God has done
from beginning to end.

ECCLESIASTES 3:11 NIV

~

These things I have written to you
who believe in the name of the Son of God,
that you may know that you have eternal life.

1 JOHN 5:13

~

Keep yourselves in the love of God, looking for the mercy
of our Lord Jesus Christ unto eternal life.

JUDE V. 21

The twists and turns of life have a way of reminding us—we aren't home here. This is not our homeland. We aren't fluent in the languages of disease and death. The culture confuses the heart, the noise disrupts our sleep, and we feel far from home.

And you know what? That's okay.

You have an eternal address fixed in your mind. God has "set eternity in the hearts of men" (Ecclesiastes 3:11 NIV). Down deep you know you are not home yet.

Traveling Light

If You Are Afraid For the Welfare of a Loved One

The Lord is not slack concerning His promise, as some count slackness, but is longsuffering toward us, not willing that any should perish but that all should come to repentance.

2 PETER 3:9

It troubled the LORD to see them in trouble, and his angel saved them. The LORD was truly merciful, so he rescued his people. He took them in his arms and carried them all those years.

ISAIAH 63:9 CEV

"I have heard your prayer, I have seen your tears."

2 KINGS 20:5

In the same way, the Spirit helps us in our weakness. We do not know what we ought to pray for, but the Spirit himself intercedes for us through wordless groans.

ROMANS 8:26 NIV

Now this is the confidence that we have in Him, that if we ask anything according to His will, He hears us. And if we know that He hears us, whatever we ask, we know that we have the petitions that we have asked of Him.

1 JOHN 5:14–15

But God demonstrates His own love toward us, in that while we were still sinners, Christ died for us.

ROMANS 5:8

Rest in the LORD, and wait patiently for Him.

PSALM 37:7

Weeping may endure for a night, but joy comes in the morning.

PSALM 30:5

Our LORD, I am praying for your servants—those you rescued by your great strength and mighty power.

NEHEMIAH 1:10 CEV

And he who searches our hearts knows the mind of the Spirit, because the Spirit intercedes for God's people in accordance with the will of God.

ROMANS 8:27 NIV

Be anxious for nothing, but in everything by prayer and supplication, with thanksgiving, let your requests be made known to God; and the peace of God, which surpasses all understanding, will guard your hearts and minds through Christ Jesus.

PHILIPPIANS 4:6–7

Therefore he is able to save completely those who come to God
through him, because he always lives to intercede for them.

HEBREWS 7:25 NIV

The LORD has heard my cry for mercy;
the Lord accepts my prayer.

PSALM 6:9 NIV

Don't worry about anything; instead, pray about
everything. Tell God what you need, and thank him for all
he has done. Then you will experience God's peace, which
exceeds anything we can understand. His peace will guard
your hearts and minds as you live in Christ Jesus.

PHILIPPIANS 4:6–7 NLT

I [Paul] have labored and toiled and have often gone
without sleep; I have known hunger and thirst and have
often gone without food; I have been cold and naked.
Besides everything else, I face daily the pressure of my
concern for all the churches. Who is weak, and I do not feel
weak? Who is led into sin, and I do not inwardly burn?

2 CORINTHIANS 11:27–29 NIV

Give all your worries and cares to
God, for he cares about you.

1 PETER 5:7 NLT

God will always give what is right to his people who cry to him night and day, and he will not be slow to answer them.

LUKE 18:7 NCV

And this is the confidence that we have in him, that, if we ask any thing according to his will, he heareth us: And if we know that he hear us, whatsoever we ask, we know that we have the petitions that we desired of him.

1 JOHN 5:14–15 KJV

But when you ask, you must believe and not doubt, because the one who doubts is like a wave of the sea, blown and tossed by the wind. That person should not expect to receive anything from the Lord.

JAMES 1:6–7 NIV

The LORD says, "This is my agreement with these people: My Spirit and my words that I give you will never leave you or your children or your grandchildren, now and forever."

ISAIAH 59:21 NCV

And we know that God causes everything to work together for the good of those who love God and are called according to his purpose for them.

ROMANS 8:28 NLT

*For the LORD will not abandon His people on
account of His great name, because the LORD has
been pleased to make you a people for Himself.*

1 SAMUEL 12:22 NASB

*I will lead the blind by ways they have not known, along
unfamiliar paths I will guide them; I will turn the darkness
into light before them and make the rough places smooth.
These are the things I will do; I will not forsake them.*

ISAIAH 42:16 NIV

*Bless the LORD, O my soul, and forget not all His benefits:
who forgives all your iniquities, who heals all your diseases,
who redeems your life from destruction, who crowns you with
lovingkindness and tender mercies, who satisfies your mouth
with good things, so that your youth is renewed like the eagle's.*

PSALM 103:2–5

*Sing to the LORD a new song, because he has done miracles.
By his right hand and holy arm he has won the victory.*

PSALM 98:1 NCV

*Let the wicked forsake his way, and the unrighteous man his
thoughts; let him return to the LORD, and He will have mercy
on him; and to our God, for He will abundantly pardon.*

ISAIAH 55:7

Evening and morning and at noon I will pray,
and cry aloud, and He shall hear my voice.

PSALM 55:17

For God is my witness, whom I serve with my spirit
in the gospel of His Son, that without ceasing I
make mention of you always in my prayers.

ROMANS 1:9

"For I will be merciful to their unrighteousness, and their
sins and their lawless deeds I will remember no more."

HEBREWS 8:12

When he has brought out all his own, he goes on ahead of
them, and his sheep follow him because they know his voice.

JOHN 10:4 NIV

The LORD has heard my supplication; the
LORD will receive my prayer.

PSALM 6:9

For we walk by faith [we regulate our lives and conduct
ourselves by our conviction or belief respecting man's
relationship to God and divine things, with trust and
holy fervor; thus we walk] not by sight or appearance.

2 CORINTHIANS 5:7 AMP

Happy is the man who has the God of Jacob as his helper, whose hope is in the Lord his God—the God who made both earth and heaven, the seas and everything in them. He is the God who keeps every promise, who gives justice to the poor and oppressed and food to the hungry. He frees the prisoners and opens the eyes of the blind.

PSALM 146:5–8 TLB

Now I commit you to God and to the word of his grace, which can build you up and give you an inheritance among all those who are sanctified.

ACTS 20:32 NIV

I thank God, whom I serve with a pure conscience, as my forefathers did, as without ceasing I remember you in my prayers night and day.

2 TIMOTHY 1:3

How precious is your constant love, O God! All humanity takes refuge in the shadow of your wings.

PSALM 36:7 TLB

God meets daily needs daily.
Not weekly or annually.
He will give you what you need
when it is needed.

Traveling Light

All of the material in this book was originally published in the following books by Max Lucado. All copyrights to the original works are held by the author, Max Lucado.

The Applause of Heaven (Nashville: Thomas Nelson, Inc., 1990).

In the Eye of the Storm (Nashville: Thomas Nelson, Inc., 1991).

He Still Moves Stones (Nashville: Thomas Nelson, Inc., 1993).

The Great House of God (Nashville: Thomas Nelson, Inc., 1997).

Just Like Jesus (Nashville: Thomas Nelson, Inc., 1998).

Traveling Light (Nashville: Thomas Nelson, Inc., 2000).

And the Angels Were Silent (Nashville: Thomas Nelson, Inc., 2003).

God Came Near (Nashville: Thomas Nelson, Inc., 2003).

Next Door Savior (Nashville: Thomas Nelson, Inc., 2003).

No Wonder They Call Him the Savior (Nashville: Thomas Nelson, Inc., 2003).

Six Hours One Friday (Nashville: Thomas Nelson, Inc., 2003).

Come Thirsty (Nashville: Thomas Nelson, Inc., 2004).

Cure for the Common Life (Nashville: Thomas Nelson, Inc., 2005).

3:16: The Numbers of Hope (Nashville: Thomas Nelson, Inc., 2007).

Every Day Deserves a Chance (Nashville: Thomas Nelson, Inc., 2007).

Fearless (Nashville: Thomas Nelson, Inc., 2009).

In the Grip of Grace (Nashville: Thomas Nelson, Inc., 1996).

A Love Worth Giving (Nashville: Thomas Nelson, Inc., 2006).